seeker, there are no new ideas here but a complete reframing. This book has simply and powerfully changed the way I live."

— Jerry L. Jackson, writer/producer/director, chair, New Members Committee, Writers Guild of America

"Inspiring, empowering, and uplifting. A heart-opening story and a great read."

— Brandon Bays, author of *The Journey*

"A great book . . . very useful and empowering."

— Ruth Ostrow, journalist, author of *Sacred & Naked*

"Move over, James Redfield! *The Magician's Way* shows just how easy it is to succeed here and now, with focus, instead of going off into the Peruvian Andes to learn. A marvelous book — I was riveted and enjoyed every page! Since reading it I sense I have made another leap forward in my journey."

— Bhagawati Morriss, metaphysical researcher, Bali

THE
MAGICIAN'S WAY

THE
MAGICIAN'S WAY

What It Really Takes to Find Your Treasure

WILLIAM WHITECLOUD

New World Library
Novato, California

New World Library
14 Pamaron Way
Novato, California
www.newworldlibrary.com

This book is a work of fiction. All names, characters, places, dialogue, and incidents portrayed are the product of the author's imagination.

Text design by Tona Pearce Myers

Library of Congress Cataloguing-in-Publication Data
Whitecloud, William.
 The magician's way : what it really takes to find your treasure / William White-cloud. — 1st New World Library ed.
    p.   cm.
Originally published in Australia in 2004.
ISBN 978-1-57731-687-9 (pbk. : alk. paper)
1. Self-realization—Fiction. I. Title.
PR9619.4.W5M34 2009
823'.92—dc22   2009027085

First New World Library edition, October 2009
ISBN 978-1-57731-687-9
Printed in Canada on 100% postconsumer-waste recycled paper

 New World Library is a proud member of the Green Press Initiative.

10 9 8 7 6 5 4 3 2 1

To my beloved wife, Christian, whose only demand on me, ever, has been that I follow my heart. Her unshakable faith in the power of love has been my greatest teacher.

CONTENTS

ACKNOWLEDGMENTS

The first chapter of this book is based on an actual experience I had with my friend Kris Barkway, author of *The New Golf Paradigm*. Kris is without a doubt the greatest exponent of magic I have ever encountered. As you would expect of a true master, Kris not only has the ability to do things that spectacularly defy belief, but more than that, he also has the ability to confer the same power on others.

PROLOGUE

My name is Mark Vale, and the one thing I can safely say about my life is that it has never been dull.

When I was growing up in Africa, every young boy kept a pet mole snake. Mole snakes are harmless little animals that, like their mammalian namesakes, live underground feeding on insects and grubs. Apart from being blind, their unique feature is that their heads are nearly indistinguishable from their tails. You really have to look carefully to tell which end is which.

All my friends had mole snakes. They were so easy to come by. You had only to turn over a rotting log or dig up a fallow vegetable patch, and there, more likely than not, would be one of these dual-headed, giant earthworm-like creatures wriggling haplessly about. Yet no matter how diligently I searched, I could never find my own pet mole snake. I was the only seven-year-old boy within a hundred miles who didn't have one.

Then one day my luck changed. I was looking for a ball that had bounced into a corn patch in our backyard when my eye caught sight of something coiled around a stalk of corn. A mole snake! Forgetting about the ball, and with my little heart beating with joy, I knelt down and put my hand out for the snake to climb onto. Up close, I noticed there was something odd about this particular mole snake. For a start it was out in the open, and it was larger and less opaque than the other mole snakes I had played with. But it had a head where its tail should have been, and it was the same dark color. I just took it to be a big daddy of a mole snake.

This little fellow wasn't as obliging as the mole snakes I was used to. It turned away from my hand and began slithering across a broad corn leaf toward another stalk. Not wanting to let it get away, I grabbed it gently around the middle and picked it up from the leaf. Before I knew it, the snake had turned around and bit my thumb. It hardly hurt at all, but I got such a fright that I flung my arm up in the air, sending the small creature flying across the sky into our neighbor's yard.

Because mole snakes are nonvenomous, I didn't feel anything except disappointment that I had lost my precious find so quickly. When you're seven years old, though, you don't hold on to disappointment for long, and I was soon kicking the ball around without a care. It wasn't till later that morning that my thumb began to throb. By lunchtime I was in real agony. When I explained to my father what had happened, his face went white as a sheet. He looked gravely at my mother, who had also turned pale, and said three words in a barely audible whisper: "Gibbons burrowing adder!"

I had heard of two people who had been bitten by burrowing adders. Both were adults. One had died. I don't know exactly how a burrowing adder's poison attacks the human physiology, but I can report firsthand on its effect. There is basically only one word to describe it: pain!

The horrible thing about being bitten by a burrowing adder is that there is no antidote. You just have to tough it out. They say that if you die from the bite, it's not the venom that kills you; it's the shock from the pain. For the next forty-eight hours, my thumb felt like it was being hit by a sledgehammer every three seconds. I didn't stop screaming for six hours, after which time the pain became so intense that I left this world, where pain was only an aspect of life, and drifted off to another world, where pain was the only thing there was.

My parents say I was unconscious for thirty-six hours, but let me tell you, I remember every moment of that living hell. I was on fire, kept awake by devils branding me all over with red-hot pokers. And my thumb, always my thumb, constantly throbbing as if it were a pain magnet drawing in every conceivable kind of agony from throughout the universe.

Obviously, I survived — otherwise you wouldn't be reading this — but there are those who say that experiences from your early life form a template from which all your later experiences emanate. I for one tend to agree with this premise. All my life I've had a consistent experience of picking things up thinking they were one thing, only to be shocked at how different they turned out to be. And this was the case in the story I am about to tell, where, many years later in another part of the world, I innocently picked up a golf club, not realizing that my life would never be the same again.

THE MAGIC GOLF LESSON

For nearly twenty years, golf had been my bête noire, my most reliable source of frustration and powerlessness. It felt personal, as though the game of golf was an entity that had it in for me, and no matter how hard I tried, it was not going to let me get anywhere.

I was on my way to the golf course for a lesson with a pro called Steve Addington, and I could feel my resentment toward the game beginning to surface. It didn't help that I was stuck without air-conditioning in traffic that was moving fifty yards every fifteen minutes on a sweltering summer afternoon. "Why on earth am I doing this?" I asked myself. I thought I'd promised myself a year ago that I'd never pick up a club again. What sort of glutton for punishment was I?

But I had to go. This golf lesson was supposedly going to save my life, and, as skeptical as I might normally be, the truth is that I was in a desperate enough situation to try

1

anything. Every wheel of my existence had begun to shudder and shake and threaten to fly off the axle. In my heart I knew that it wouldn't be long before everything I lived for was torn from my grasp and lost to me forever.

Some years back, my wife, Kirsten, and I had decided to leave the city and move to an idyllic coastal community ten hours' drive north. Our logic was that, because my business selling independent financial trends analysis was global and conducted almost exclusively on the phone, we could live anywhere in the world we wanted. Kirsten had chosen to put aside her aspiration to become an interior designer and had concentrated her energies on being a full-time mother to our two young children. Furthermore, with the equity we raised from selling our pokey townhouse, we could buy a substantial property in the country and pay the same mortgage as we did in the city. We imagined ourselves living a peaceful life far away from the manic pace of the city, settled in a spacious country manor surrounded by a sea of bucolic tranquillity. There would be chickens in the yard, we told each other, fruit trees laden with exotic offerings, and horses coming up at sunset to nibble oats out of our hands. There would be days at the beach; small, personalized classrooms for our children when they reached school age; a guest cottage for our best friends to stay in; and a relaxed, friendly, abundant environment for us to grow closer in. And of course, what a gift to our children it would be, providing them with a safe, wonder-filled world to grow up in.

It wasn't difficult to convince ourselves, and to the surprise and dismay of our friends and relatives, we sold our townhouse and moved to the country, where we did buy the country mansion surrounded by acres of dams and rivers and orchards and English-style cottage gardens. But somehow the dream never materialized. We had all the ingredients, but the cake didn't rise — the quality of life we'd imagined never came to be.

Country life, we were horrified to discover, wasn't just a look or an image; it was hard work. Noxious weeds needed management, trees needed water, animals needed feeding, gardens needed attention, fruit had to be picked, roads fixed, pipes mended, pumps serviced, grass slashed. We were trapped on a bigger treadmill than the one we'd just escaped. Everything we did was a race against time. If animals weren't fed, they starved; if plants didn't get water, they died; if vegetation wasn't cut back, it overran the place; if things weren't fixed early, they ended up creating untold havoc.

We were run off our feet from the crack of dawn to the middle of the night, and in between we tried to run a business, care for our children, and have some kind of an intimate relationship. Even the pleasures of life became a chore. We had to drag ourselves to the beach or to a romantic night out. Where once Kirsten and I had been paragons of wedded bliss, our relationship at first deteriorated until we were simply allies in a losing battle, and then finally to a point where each suspected the other of being the enemy.

The remedy to our ill-fated move seemed simple, but moving back to the city wouldn't have been as easy as it sounded. Our problem was that in the years we had been living in the country, the price of property in the city had virtually doubled, while values where we had bought were weak. We couldn't afford to move back to the city — not without losing what to us represented a fortune. The only solution, as I saw it, was to make more money. If we made more money, then we could pay others to do the menial chores that robbed us of the gentrified life we had originally envisioned.

There were two snags to this solution. The first was that to make more money I had to dedicate more time to my business, which meant Kirsten was left to deal with the unwanted burdens on her own. The harder I worked, the more she saw me as the real enemy — never mind that I was working for our mutual benefit.

To make matters worse, the gold mine I'd been lazily mining for the previous seven years had begun to dry up. Business conditions had become tough. Not only had the Internet and online search and delivery services undermined my clients' dependence on me for the most reliable information, but also the global financial slowdown meant that the organizations' budgets for external analysis had been cut back to the bone. It now cost me three times as much money as before, and that much more time, to make a dollar in the prevailing business conditions.

I was in a terrible fix. I would have to work the phones more diligently to survive, and I would also have to begin traveling again to shore up support where I had it and create it where I didn't. It was the only thing I could think of. At the same time, I knew there would be nothing to come back to if I went down that road. I would be doomed if I acted and doomed if I didn't.

I felt absolutely desperate. I couldn't imagine a life without money. I couldn't imagine a life without my family. It just seemed inevitable that a fate worse than death was slowly overtaking me. At sunset I'd watch my little boy and girl run down to the neighbors' fence and feed their horses sugar cubes. How sweet their laughter was, how complete their happiness was, how certain they were that life was only pregnant with wonderful possibility. Little could they suspect that our circumstances were squeezing the air out of that blessed life. And, even more tragically, that the only way I could conceive of improving our circumstances would make things even worse.

Now here I was, back in the city I had spurned, going from door to door with my cap in hand, doing what I could to keep the source of my life from drying up completely. I was staying with my old friend Cliff Bannister, the man who had originally persuaded me to get out of money market trading and into selling the information that financial market operatives depended on, a move that had, until recently, been one I had not regretted. One of the first people to call on me at Cliff's stylish inner-city townhouse was another old friend and money market colleague, Kaye Lerner, who had by now graduated to being an associate director with one of the city's most prominent investment banks. Since Kirsten and I had moved to the country, Kaye had been our most frequent visitor and knew us in our latest incarnation better than anyone else. I had only to tell her the scantest

details of our predicament before Kaye insisted I take the
time to have a lesson with Steve Addington while I was
in town. "I know how much you hate golf, Mark," she
allowed. "But this isn't about golf; this man will teach you
something that will change your life completely. It's a technique for succeeding at everything you undertake."

When I pressed Kaye for more details, she wasn't forth-
coming. "I can't explain it, Mark. It's something you have to
experience. You won't believe it unless you actually try it."

I doubt I would have gone to see Steve on Kaye's vague
say-so alone, but everyone I spoke to seemed to have had a
lesson with Steve and raved about it as if it were a religious
experience. Even my nongolfing friends were going to see
him for the sheer inspiration of the experience. In the end,
it was my own desperation that convinced me. If he was half
as good as everyone promised, I had to see him. It wasn't
about golf, I knew; but the fact that golf was the vehicle
really made me cranky.

By the time I got to the driving range, I was in a state.
Thanks to the rush-hour traffic, I was late, tense, and uncomfortably hot. The prospect of hacking ineffectually at
golf balls for the remainder of the day didn't do anything to
lift my mood. I was feeling prickly. This Steve guy was on
short probation. The first sign that this was the same old
"practice this shot till you're a hundred and you'll get there
in the end," and I was out of there. I was here for one thing
only: the radical result I'd been promised.

It was in Steve's favor that he turned out to be an easy-
going young guy with a pleasant smile that said, "Hey, this

isn't life or death. We're just going to have some fun." Many of the golf pros I'd sought enlightenment from previously had the attitude that golf was an implacable enemy, and that if they didn't impress on me how seriously I had to take their training, then the battle was lost. Steve's attitude seemed to be that golf was a joke, and that, no matter what, the last laugh would always be on the game, not us. Quickly, I realized there was something unusual about this man. It didn't matter if you were on time or late, or whether you hit a good shot or a bad shot — life was about something else to him.

Every time I started with any pro, the first thing he or she did was get me to hit a few balls to see how I swung the club and then point out what I was doing wrong, and so began the long road to correcting my action. The pro either widened or narrowed my stance and got me to flex or straighten my knees, keep the left arm straight, drop the right shoulder, put the weight on the right foot and then transfer to the left, keep my eye on the ball, and so on. Then would begin the monotony of practicing each of these aspects for hours on end. And just as I'd begin getting one thing right, something else would go off. So it was an endless process of finding a corrective technique and practicing it, finding another corrective technique and practicing that.

With Steve it was different. Same as the other pros, he handed me an eight iron, asked me to hit a few shots, and nodded sagely as I sliced a couple into a foursome teeing off on a fairway to our right, skulled another ball that dribbled off the edge of the practice tee, and then hooked a couple more into the forest on our left. Immediately I felt that sickening sense of hopelessness come over me and looked to Steve for the correction that would have me hitting sweet lofted shots straight down the fairway. But Steve wasn't interested in my style at all.

"What were you aiming at?" he asked.

"Nothing," I replied. "I was just concentrating on hitting a good shot."

"Well, there you go. That's why you don't play good golf," remarked Steve casually.

"But you have to hit a good shot to play good golf," I retorted in that tone that accuses the other person of being an idiot.

"Sure you do," Steve agreed amicably. "Just like you have to throw a good throw to hit that tree over there." He turned and lobbed a ball at a slender gum tree standing fifty feet away from us. The ball hit the tree midway up the trunk. "Try that," he said, holding out a ball to me. I didn't know what he was getting at, but I was happy to oblige. Because I grew up on a farm in Africa, throwing stones was second nature to me, as it was a skill every country boy took seriously and practiced all the time. Putting down my club, I threw the golf ball at the tree. Bang. It hit the trunk in about the same spot Steve's throw had hit it.

"Good shot," he cried out, very pleased. "Try again."

I threw four or five more balls at the tree, all of them either hitting the mark or just missing.

"Wow, you can really throw," beamed Steve with genuine admiration. Then his tone changed to one of serious interest. "So tell me, when you threw the balls at that tree, what were you thinking about?"

It sounded like a trick question. I wasn't sure what to say. "Nothing," I answered guardedly.

"Were you conscious of how you were holding the ball?"

"No."

"Were you conscious about bringing your arm back? Your wrist movement?"

"No."

"Shifting your weight from your back foot to your front foot?"

"No."

"Okay," said Steve, "go back to your last throw and feel where your focus is as you throw the ball. What's in your mind as you throw the ball? What can you see?"

"The target," I answered, realizing consciously for the first time that when I throw at a target my mind sees only the very center of that target, as if I'm holding a magnifying glass up to it.

"Exactly!" exclaimed Steve. "You're connected with your target. You're one with the target. And that's what golf is about. The target. People are taught that it's about the swing, that if they get the swing right then they'll hit the target. But that's not true. It's the other way around. If they focus on the target, they'll inevitably hit a good shot."

Steve stopped talking and took a good look around us as if he wanted to make sure no one else was listening. I had the feeling he was about to let me in on a big secret. "You see," he began again in a hushed tone, "everything you've been taught about golf is a big myth. It's driven by fear — the fear that we can't hit a golf ball. Consequently, we don't rely on our natural ability. We try to control the shot with our rational minds.

"When you're playing a shot, you're standing in an invisible circle. Golfers believe that you hit a good shot by getting everything in the circle right, that if you can simultaneously control every aspect of the swing, then it will translate to getting the ball to do what you want it to. But golf is really about what's outside the circle. It's about the target. If you can go back to trusting your natural ability and just focus on the target, you'll play excellent golf. You'll be able to do anything you want."

Mmmmmhhh ... That sounded impressive in theory. I nodded and grunted appreciatively while Steve spoke, but I was skeptical. Throwing a golf ball or a stone at a target was a relatively simple task. It would compare to the complexity of golf only if you had to hit a target by throwing a small object at another small object and strike the second object so precisely that it was propelled in exactly the right direction with exactly the right amount of power. In golf, you're dealing with an intermediary object that's subject to an infinite number of variables. Hitting a tree by throwing something at it is easy. Hitting a golf ball is easy, too. Hitting it so that it lands precisely where you want it to land a hundred and fifty yards away is another story.

If Steve was aware of my skepticism, he didn't show it.

"Let's try out what I'm talking about," he suggested, setting about ten balls up in a row on the practice tee.

"We'll use the same tree as a target. What I want you to do is walk up to each ball, look at the tree, mentally acknowledge it as the target, look down at the ball, and then hit it, but don't think about your swing. Keep thinking about where you want the ball to go. It's just like throwing a stone. Just stay connected to the target."

I approached the nearest ball tentatively and stood over it, nervously adjusting my stance and grip and aim, wriggling the club about and practicing a few back swings. I looked at the tree, and for the first time ever got a sense of how intimidating it was to commit to such a defined target. I quickly retreated into the comfort of my swing circle and concentrated on looking at the ball and thinking of taking the clubhead back slowly, letting it fall, and keeping my head down. And somewhere in there I thought briefly of the tree. There was a big thud as my clubhead dug into the ground behind the ball, and a tremendous shock rippled up my right forearm, almost dislocating my shoulder.

"Holy cow!" marveled Steve. "Man, you're trying to hit that ball as if the target is about three hundred yards away. It's only thirty or so feet away. Just relax. Don't worry about the swing. Just keep imagining where you want the ball to go."

The first ball was still sitting smugly on the tee Steve had placed it on. I began addressing it very deliberately again. "Don't fuss about," Steve cut in. "Just stand next to the ball. Look at the tree. Look at the ball. And hit it. All the time, keep the tree in mind. Don't worry about your stance, your direction, nothing. Let go."

I tried it again. I found that my mind still wanted to cling to the old focus, but at the same time I managed to hold my vision of the target better than I had on the last swing. The shot felt a lot more relaxed, and to my surprise there was a sweet-sounding "ping" and the golf ball jumped out at the little gum tree, missing it by a whisker. I went down the line of balls Steve had set up, doing my best to employ his technique. The results were mixed, but I had a definite sense that when I hit a sweet shot I was connected with the target, and when I hit a duffer I was trapped in my swing circle again.

Steve was encouraging. He could tell I felt the difference. "Okay," he laughed, "you've got it. Now, let's really get you out of your head." He looked up from the end of a new row of balls he had lined up. "This time don't spend any time over the ball. Don't think for a second. Just walk up to it. Look at the target. Lock it in. Look at the ball and hit. Keep the target in mind." I was a little self-conscious at first, but after a couple of balls I was just clipping them without any concern about negative consequences. To hell with it; the ball could go wherever it wanted. I was just going to do exactly what Steve suggested. To my surprise, the balls went sailing toward the target. None of them actually hit the tree, but they all lobbed nicely into the air and fell in a tight pattern around the base of the tree.

A few of the shots felt awkward. I caught myself thinking that the clubface was too open or that my right arm wasn't far enough away from my ribs. But whatever came into my mind, I didn't let it take my attention away from my vision of where I wanted the ball to go. Without having to worry how my swing was going, I relaxed mentally, and, correspondingly, I could feel that my swing was nice and easy. It felt really good to be hitting balls by deciding where I wanted them to go rather than by trying to force them. After five minutes with Steve, I was having fun — something I hadn't associated with golf for decades.

Steve was beaming one of those "How amazing is this?" smiles. He was already satisfied that he had shattered another golfer's mythology. I had chipped only twenty balls, and I was converted to the mystic's approach. He set up another ten balls, and I joyfully whacked them off their tees, feeling the thrill of each true shot vibrate through my whole body. Every ball sailed through the air, seemingly guided by my will. I felt as if I could do no wrong, as if I were one with the game. It was an incredibly good feeling.

I helped Steve set up another row of balls. "Okay," he said, "let's make it a little more interesting. You see the forked tree over there?" He pointed to a medium-sized gum tree on the edge of the practice fairway about forty yards away. "Try hitting the balls through the fork of the tree."

I stood over the first ball and looked at the target. I swallowed. Two spindly branches grew vertically from the top of the tree trunk. The branches reached about thirty feet into the air and were about three feet apart at the widest point. That was my target. Once again, I was made conscious of how uncomfortable I was taking on such a narrowly defined objective. The longer I looked at the target, the closer to-gether the two branches seemed to grow and the more clearly my own sense of powerlessness and incapability came into focus. I hit all ten balls employing the technique Steve had taught me, but with the hopeless conviction that I couldn't do it. Each shot was a shocker. The balls went everywhere except near the tree I was aiming for. I felt sick. The magic had evaporated, and the curse of eternal defeat weighed on me as heavily as ever.

Steve wasn't at all fazed. He just stood there looking right through me. There was an awkward silence, and when at last he spoke, I realized he'd been reading my mind. "You don't believe you can do it, do you?" he asked.

"No," I admitted, my shoulders hunched in defeat. I was angry with myself for persisting with something I had well and truly proved I couldn't do.

Steve spoke again with a clarity that snapped me out of my pessimistic frame of mind. "That's fine. It doesn't mat-ter what you do, as long as you're honest with me. As long as we go for the truth, then you'll be able to take back con-trol again. You have to be able to see where you are before you can see where you want to be. You're just back in the swing circle now. If you see this, then you'll be able to go back to the target. Then you'll hit great shots again. Okay?"

I nodded.

"Good. The thing to do now is just acknowledge that you don't believe you can do it. You look at the target, and you don't know how you can hit it. You have no confidence in your natural ability, so you come back to the swing circle.

Problem is, I've taken away your tools for forcing the shot. You're not allowed to focus on the swing. So, as you hit the balls, where does your focus go? What do you see?"

"The target?" I ventured lamely.

"If it was the fork in the tree, the balls would have gone through the fork. Think about it. Close your eyes and go back to each shot. Notice what you're seeing in your mind. Where do you really see the ball going?"

I closed my eyes and thought about the shots. I was surprised to realize that while I did think of the target superficially, at a deeper level there was a stronger picture of the balls being pulled off target by some magnetic force opposing my will. "All over the place," I confessed gladly, the insight giving me a renewed sense of hope.

"And where did we see the balls go out there?" asked Steve, raising his eyebrows to indicate that we both knew the answer to his question. "So what I want you to do now is just acknowledge that you don't believe you can do it. Once you do that, your mind doesn't have to spend energy coping with your negative belief. Your attention can move on from the swing circle. You can be free to concentrate on the target again."

I eagerly helped Steve tee up the next row of balls and approached my first shot with renewed conviction. But before I had a chance to even look up at the V-shaped eucalyptus, Steve had another suggestion for me.

"Okay, Mark, what you want to do is become the ball. Be the ball floating through the fork. When you become one with your end result, your natural ability will pull everything together to create that result. Just try that now without hitting a ball. Just imagine the ball floating over the fork. Better still, be the ball doing what you want it to do."

I tried doing what he said, but in my mind the ball didn't want to go through the branches. Steve could tell by the look on my face that it wasn't happening for me.

"The problem is that you're too attached to the outcome. Your mind is making it a matter of life and death. It's like you'll imagine it only if you know for certain that it can happen. That means you're still inside the swing circle trying to control it. You have to get out of the swing circle and out to the target. You can't do that if you've got a big investment in the outcome. Your trouble is that you have a fear of failure. Let go of whether it will happen or not. Remember, it's just a game. And the game isn't about a good result or a bad result; the game is in imagining the ball doing what you want it to. Play that game — the imagination game."

I tried again, this time not focusing on what I felt would happen in reality. I acknowledged that I thought the likely outcome of my next shot would be bad and allowed that possibility to exist. It was like cutting an albatross from around my neck. Immediately, my spirits soared and I was able to imagine anything I wanted. In my mind I sent the ball whistling through the branches or drifting high and slow over the tree. Again I was one with what I wanted, not with my negative belief.

"So this time," said Steve, interrupting my pleasant reverie, "what I want you to do is hold that vision of the ball going through the fork. Acknowledge the target, and then, all the way through your swing, keep imagining the ball sailing through the fork. And to help you with that, I want you to hit the ball with your eyes closed."

"What?" I didn't believe my ears. You could argue about stance and grip and things like that, but everyone knew that the absolute foundation of a good shot was keeping your head down and your eye on the ball. Could I have heard right? Was this lunatic asking me to give up my last shred of control? What control would I have if I couldn't even see the ball? I felt all wobbly just thinking about it.

"Just look at the target. Look down at the ball. Close your eyes and hit it. Just keep imagining the ball sailing through the fork in the tree," Steve said evenly. He walked away from the practice tee, and suddenly it felt like I was out there by myself.

Being left alone like that gave me a great sense of freedom. I felt like I could stretch my imagination as far as I wanted. I could let myself dream. I squared up to the first ball again without fussing about my line. I looked at the forked tree and stood there imagining the ball floating through the middle of the gap. Then I looked down at the ball and closed my eyes. There was an instant when I suddenly felt lost to the ball, disoriented, but I just went back to imagining myself as the ball gliding over the target. With my eyes closed, the V opened up into a wide fork that I sailed through effortlessly. I was only vaguely aware of some corner of my mind saying, "This feels weird. I don't feel coordinated enough." I was so focused on the target that the swing was happening with little conscious effort.

As I struck the ball, I knew it was a sweet shot. Every fiber of my body tingled exquisitely. Even the sound of the club connecting with the ball left a musical note ringing in my ears. I opened my eyes to see the ball arching crisply through the air toward my ambitious little target. The ball cleared the tree about five feet above and slightly to the left of the V.

"Man, what a beautiful shot!" cried Steve, expressing my own sentiment perfectly.

I stepped up to the next ball and hit it with my eyes closed again. Same result: beautiful shot; beautiful sensation; missed the target by a whisker. As I went down the line hitting the balls, there was always the same curious resistance in the back of my mind that would melt away as soon as I struck the ball. It was as though a piece of driftwood caught in an eddy were suddenly carried off by the main current of a swollen river. There was that moment at impact when everything was swallowed up and carried off by the vision.

When you hit a great golf shot, the thrill is unique. But when you hit a ball with your eyes closed and it turns out to be the best shot you've ever hit in your life, the emotional response is pure euphoria. On the fifth shot the ball cut the V in half. Had there been a bull's-eye between those two branches, I would have hit it. As I watched the ball drifting lazily beyond the tree, I suddenly became aware of my follow-through posture. I was even more amazed. I knew my finish was perfect. If I could have seen myself, I would have looked like a pro on TV.

"Now you're letting go. Now you're letting go," Steve sang out.

"That's incredible," I marveled. "Look at how I finished up. My weight is on my front foot. I never transfer my weight."

"Man, that was a perfect swing." Steve sounded as if he'd just witnessed a once-in-a-lifetime event. "That's what I said, though, isn't it? If you focus on the target, everything else comes together. But if you think about ending up with your body facing the target and transferring your weight and using timing instead of force, you'll end up tied up in knots and hit an ordinary shot."

His words were horribly prophetic. The next two shots were ordinary. They didn't stray too far from the target, but they just felt awful and had none of the vibrancy or grace of the five preceding shots.

"There you go," laughed Steve, evidently happy that his premise was so predictable. "Now you're thinking of how you should be finishing up. You're back in the swing circle. Your enemy is expectation. Your ally is detachment. The game isn't the process; the game is the dream."

Several times now after I had messed up, Steve had encouraged me to replay the shot in my mind and observe what was actually going on in my consciousness as I hit the ball. I did that now voluntarily and saw that, in fact, my attention was now partly on getting the finish right. I let that go and went back to concentrating on where I wanted the balls to go. What do you know? The next three shots made my heart sing.

I hit another thirty balls at the same target. All but a couple of shots were just brilliant. What a joy it was to open my eyes and see the ball decisively following the path I had chosen for it. More than anything, my euphoria was created by the sense that I could will the impossible to happen. It was an incredible feeling of power, the realization that I could cause reality to turn into what I wanted it to be. I was connected to my magic.

Steve couldn't wipe the smile off his face. I could feel how happy he was, too. It was obvious that his bliss came from shattering people's assumptions around process orientation and revealing the secret of effortless manifestation to them. Nothing would give him more pleasure, I was sure, than sharing the magical parallel universe he lived in.

Steve's job wasn't too difficult, either. There wasn't much for him to do other than make admiring comments about my shots and whoop whenever I put the ball through the slot. His favorite cry was "Now you're letting go. Now you're letting go." As a coach, all he had to do was reinforce the rule that my focus was the only thing determining what the ball did. On the odd occasion that I hit a stray shot, Steve would simply get me to replay the shot in my mind and allow myself to see everything I was thinking and feeling. One time I hit a shocking slice that landed ninety degrees to our right on an adjoining fairway. "What the heck were you focused on then?" cried Steve in a tone of genuine awe.

"The target," I replied, totally bamboozled. As far as I was aware, I'd done everything right.

"Well, let's rerun it in your mind. If you take yourself through the shot again, what stands out?"

"When I closed my eyes, I saw a group of golfers who were on the fairway before I hit the shot," I told Steve.

"And before you hit that shot, you thought, 'I mustn't hit those people,' didn't you?"

"That's what I thought."

"Even though they were way off target."

"Yup."

Steve indulged himself with a little smile and shake of the head. He was enjoying the integrity of his premise. "That's your fear taking over, you see. Your mind suddenly recognizes the potential for embarrassment or disaster. You're either going to hit a shot that'll look bad in front of those people, or, even worse, you'll hit one of them and get sued by the lawyer in their party."

Everything Steve said left me in no doubt that he was a mind reader.

"So then," he continued, "there's a conflict between your vision and the part of you that doesn't trust your natural ability. If your fear is stronger than your vision, you're going to go back to the swing circle and try to control the outcome. When you're in the swing circle, the outcome will more closely resemble what you fear than what you want. The interesting thing is that by the time you played that shot, the group had moved on. But the fear had been triggered. It was still hanging about. When you hit the ball, you were still thinking, 'I mustn't mess this shot up.' In fact, the strongest picture in your mind was where the ball shouldn't go. And where did the ball end up?"

"Exactly where I didn't want it to go," I acknowledged, the truth of what Steve was saying sinking into my bone marrow.

"It's the same with water and bunkers," said Steve. "You look at them and say, 'I mustn't go there,' and when you hit the ball, you're subconsciously holding a picture of the hazard in your mind. It's all in the mind. The last message the mind gets determines the result out there. That's why you can't just imagine where you want the ball to go; you have to be conscious of what other messages you're giving yourself. You've got to acknowledge fear, doubt — any kind of limitation. We try to overrule the negative, to control it. That just locks us up in the swing circle. You have to learn to love the negative; you have to welcome it, because when you can see it you can take the power out of it. You can let it go.

"The key to letting go is vulnerability. Fear is resistance to a negative outcome. You don't want something to happen. You're not going to let it happen, so you take control away from your natural ability. That locks you in the swing circle. There you are, trying to get everything right; meanwhile, you're totally stiff with fear. On the other hand, as I've said before, if you can be open to the worst happening, then you're free. If it's okay to hit a bad shot, then you have no business in the swing circle. You can concentrate on the target."

At this point, Steve chuckled at some image in his own mind. "Fear is like a well-meaning but useless friend. It's trying to protect you from something going wrong. It locks you down, stops your flow. You have to keep yourself open, keep flowing. You do that by allowing the worst to happen. So don't just lock yourself on the target; be aware of what's going on in your head."

Before I hit the next ball, I took a moment to notice my thoughts and feelings. The awful slice had rattled my confidence. Even though I'd hit a dozen perfect shots before the bad one, I was suddenly unconvinced that I had it in me to produce a magical shot again. I let myself imagine hitting a pathetic shot and then affirmed to myself that this was an acceptable possibility. That might happen, I thought, but the game I'm playing is imagining a great shot and hitting it — with my eyes closed! There was a sweet, egg-cracking noise, and the ball went sailing through the V. I looked at Steve. He was jumping up and down with his arms in the air as if he himself had hit a hole in one at the U.S. Masters.

After that, Steve had me hitting balls full-strength over a grove of big blue gum trees about a hundred yards away. Every shot was sweeter than the last. I could have stood there all evening lofting balls over the trees. But I felt ready for something more advanced.

"So, how do you hook or draw a ball?" I asked Steve.

"Same way," he replied. "You just imagine it. Try that now."

I thought hitting the ball with my eyes closed was my last barrier, but I was obviously wrong. I was more attached to technique than I realized. It was one thing to hit a straightforward shot intuitively, but in my book here were some things that called for technical procedure, like drawing the ball from right to left or fading it from left to right. As I stood there trying to imagine the ball curving through the air, I couldn't help falling back on trying to remember what I had been taught about the hook shot: face the direction you want the ball to take off on, and hold your club face in the direction you want the ball to land. Surprising myself, I still hit a good shot, except it went dead straight. There was no spin on it at all.

Steve let me hit a few more balls. "You don't believe you can do it without the technique, do you?" he said matter-of-factly.

"No."

"Same principle," he shrugged. "Let's just say my way doesn't work. So we're not trying to draw the ball, okay? You don't know how to draw a ball. So we're just going to imagine that it happens — it doesn't actually have to happen. Try that without hitting it. Just imagine."

As soon as my end result didn't have to happen, I was easily able to imagine the ball curving through the air. "Okay, now imagine becoming the ball drawing through the air." That, too, was easy. I was the ball flying over a big gum and banking to the left. There was nothing of me in the swing circle. When Steve could sense I was flowing again, he said, "Now just do that and hit the ball. No expectations, though."

Addressing a loose ball lying on the practice tee, I imagined the curved path I wanted it to take, and then I looked down at the ball and closed my eyes. As I swung, I kept imagining I was the flight of the ball. There was an especially delicious egg-cracking noise. I felt sensational even before I opened my eyes. I kept them closed for a second longer than usual, then opened them to see the ball rising up into the air. My heart sank for a moment as the ball kept on going in a straight line, then soared again as the ball climbed up over the gum trees and began peeling off to the left. It seemed to hang in the air for a time and then drift down onto the circle of dark green grass I had imagined it landing on.

Steve's excitement had peaked with the last shot I'd hit through the forked gum tree. Now he just let his bottom jaw fall and stood there with his mouth open in feigned disbelief. I continued practicing the draw, hooking the ball more and more radically with every shot until I was satisfied it was something I could do at will.

There was still one technique I wanted Steve to help me with: the secret of hitting a number-one driver. When I asked Steve to teach me, he looked at me for a while to gauge whether I was joking.

"You're serious," he laughed. "Holy cow, man, don't you get it? It's the same for everything. What? Do you think your natural ability can play irons but not woods? Do you think it can hook but not fade? Come on, what you learned today is everything you need to know. There isn't anything in life you can't do with what I taught you today."

And that was the end of the lesson. There was nothing more to discuss.

THE TRICK OF THE MIND

Driving to my golf lesson with Steve, I'd been crawling through that midafternoon traffic created by motorists trying to get out of the city to avoid the end-of-day rush hour. Driving back to Cliff's home, I was caught in the real thing. With the heat of the day pressed to the earth by a blanket of carbon monoxide, it was like sitting in a toxic oven. But this time the unhappy prospect of languishing in a river of exhaust fumes with a sweat-soaked shirt clinging to my back didn't affect me too badly at all. Inside, I was very cool.

I'd arrived at the golf lesson fully enclosed in my swing circle, fighting all the forces that seemed to limit and control me: the traffic, golf, even my own inabilities. If they didn't exist or if I could control them, then I would be okay, I believed. But my powerlessness over my unwanted realities had kept me locked up in an experience of disappointment and resentment.

By the time I left Steve, I was standing fully outside my swing circle, back in my power. It didn't matter what my circumstances were. They might not be pleasant, but I didn't have to fear them like before. I was living in a world where everything was invisibly coming together to produce the life I would love to live. There was nothing I could do about the snail-paced traffic, the baking heat, or the filthy air I was breathing. But I could let life carry me forward in its own way and at its own pace to a reality of my choosing. I imagined being showered and fresh, feeling good in a clean change of clothes, and sipping a glass of chilled white wine in the cool courtyard of my host's backyard, among old friends celebrating each other's company. That was where I was going; that was what I wanted.

And then the most amazing thing happened. It was as if an express lane appeared out of nowhere for my own private use. I wasn't stuck there in a standoff with another driver over who had the right-of-way, or cursing a car that had doomed me to wait for another change of lights by cutting in front of me. I was weaving in and out of traffic effortlessly, somehow always in the lane that was moving or being signaled to cut into a free-flowing lane by some gracious driver. By some miracle, the momentum never stopped. I was flowing smoothly forward, the relaxed and positive frame of mind I expected in the future becoming a reality in the moment.

What I'd learned from Steve, which was immediately validated on my way home, was that I didn't need to control myself or the world around me to create what I wanted in life — I only had to control my attitude. I could fight golf and traffic all I wanted, using up my energy in the process, but my experience of them wouldn't change much. Or I could simply change my attitude, change what I was focused on, and end up with an entirely different end result — the one I wanted to have.

Later, when I was showered and fresh and was mingling with the old friends Cliff had reunited in honor of my visit, I was taken aside by Kaye, who had personally organized my lesson with Steve. "How was it?" she squealed, letting me know with a squeeze of my arm that she wanted to hear everything. I obliged her with an enthusiastic report, which I concluded by marveling, "It's just amazing how you can struggle with something all your life and then one day be blessed enough to discover the secret that turns the whole world upside down and gives you what you want in an instant."

Kaye was one of my oldest friends and confidants, as was evidenced by her warm and contented smile. "You see everyone here?" She waved her cocktail glass at the assembled company. "Everyone here belongs to the same club. They all live what you learned today. You look at them, and you don't notice anything different. Some of them are rich, a few are famous, and some of us are of more modest means and reputation." Kaye, the high-profile investment banker, let her own modesty sink in. "What you can't see is the ease with which all our friends here live. You can't see the joy they experience every day. That's why we were all so keen for you to see Steve. And by the looks of it, it has paid off." She clinked her glass against mine.

"They're all golfers?" I said, surprised.

"Not all," replied Kaye, "but we all play the game Steve teaches."

I looked around at my old friends with a new respect. I was surrounded by celebrated artists, gifted healers, accomplished musicians, and some of the shrewdest businesspeople in the city. I felt privileged to be initiated into their "game," as Kaye called it. Knowing their secret, though, made me feel like a novice, a humble beginner at a table of masters.

Kaye squeezed my arm again to bring my attention back to her. "There's someone I've brought along with me for you to meet," she said. "Have you heard of Trevor Campbell?"

Trevor Campbell was a legend. He had recently won the world futures-trading championship for the fourth time. I also knew of Trevor because he was a client of mine; I'd sold him several commodity-forecasting subscriptions, but I'd never met him in the flesh. I tended to be a little apprehensive about meeting my clients in person, perhaps fearing that I wouldn't be able to project the aura of authority I did over the phone.

My clients were senior executives in major corporations and government departments around the world and, for the most part, highly switched-on individuals with little time or tolerance for anyone not on their level of competence or expertise. Holding their attention — let alone enthusing them about my product — was a nerve-racking occupation. One slip and the phone line would go dead.

For all his awesome reputation, Trevor Campbell turned out to be a down-to-earth human being whom I immediately felt at ease with and took a great liking to. Rather tall and sallow-faced with a shock of jet-black hair that didn't know whether it wanted to stand up or lie down, Trevor initially gave the impression that he was the ignorant party in whatever topic was being discussed. No matter how trivial the conversation, he always listened appreciatively, as though he had a lot to gain by absorbing every word. Trevor made you feel your contribution was a unique and valuable insight into whatever subject was being discussed. As he listened, with his head cocked, he would grunt appreciatively and dig for more information with enthusiastic questions. He took a genuine interest.

Kaye maneuvered Trevor and me into a deserted area of the courtyard and made the introductions. Trevor broke into a happy smile that I was surprised to see on a face as intense as his. "Aha! My supplier," he exclaimed, ignoring my outstretched hand and embracing me in a warm bear hug. "This is my information man," he said to Kaye, still keeping me locked in his python embrace. There was a strong sense of camaraderie in his gesture; it communicated that we were not just remote acquaintances but brothers-in-arms in the same glorious quest.

"Mine, too," laughed Kaye, and then, when Trevor finally released me from his brotherly hold, she mentioned my lesson with Steve.

"Aaah!" said Trevor, raising his eyebrows. "That's interesting. How did you find it?"

"Amazing," I replied, and went on to describe my experience with childlike enthusiasm. The look of fascination on Trevor's face emboldened me to brag with childish pride how I'd even used Steve's visioning technique to cut through the rush-hour traffic on my way back from the session.

"Fantastic. Fantastic." Trevor shook his head in wonder. "Isn't it incredible how the law of focus applies to everything?"

"Trevor is the master of focus," said Kaye, a touch of friendly flattery and professional respect combining in her voice. "That's the key to your trading success, isn't it, Trevor?"

"Well," said Trevor, coughing modestly, "there isn't much else to it. You know, there was a magician called Assam who lived in Persia about a thousand years ago. And he said that in his experience 98 percent of people used their minds to create poverty and misery, while only 2 percent used their minds to create fun and profit. Not many people realize that there's a trick to success in life, a trick of the mind. It's all in the mind." Trevor gave a weak smile that apologized for burdening us with his theories. Kaye urged him on with a forceful nod.

"You see," Trevor went on, "for most people, success and failure are accidental, in the sense that they don't consciously know what determines either. Most people think there's a right way to do something, and they believe that if they can do it the right way and the conditions are right, then they'll succeed. At the same time, they believe that if they don't get it exactly right and the conditions aren't conducive, then they'll fail. In other words, 98 percent of human beings believe that ability and circumstance are the determinants of success in every instance and aspect of life.

"If we use your traffic analogy, Mark, you'll see that we assume that to get from A to B in a car efficiently, we need to be good drivers behind the wheel of a reliable car in favorable traffic conditions. Makes sense, doesn't it? I know I'd rather be in a car with a sober driver on a clear road than with a drunk driver in holiday traffic. The problem is that we take the aspects of ability and circumstance and make them absolutely responsible for every outcome in life. We don't appreciate that there's an element that has the power to override our linear reality.

"We take that limited belief system and think that in order to earn a good living, we need to select the right vocation, get good qualifications, and then, if the economy is good, get a job and do it well. We believe if we do all that and the job market is with us, we'll prosper. Ability and circumstance. We limit possibility to how proficient we are with our rational mind and physical body, and also to the prevailing conditions.

"I mean, as you know, I trade futures, and in my business you see the proof of what I'm talking about. It most probably has the biggest ratio of losers to winners of any activity in the world, including straight gambling. Statistically, heroin addicts have a better chance of getting clean than futures traders have of making money consistently."

"Why is that?" asked Kaye.

"Well," said Trevor, "it's impossible to predict micromovements in the markets, which is what you're doing when you trade futures. Simple as that. As Mark was describing, there are many factors that come together to make a golf swing; similarly, there are so many factors influencing the price of a commodity, both fundamental and psychological, that it's impossible to know and quantify them all. So you're operating in an environment where the slightest error costs you a fortune, and you can't be sure which way the market is going to move next in the short term.

"Futures traders are afraid that they can't make money doing what they do; they're conditioned to believe that the market is beyond their ability. Like you were saying, golfers don't believe they can hit a ball; traders don't believe they can pick a market. As a result, they believe that things like cash preservation strategies, how much capital you have, how well informed you are, and finding the most reliable technical model determine success."

Basically Trevor had covered everything I believed to be important in market speculation. "But don't you need to have systems and strategies?" I ventured.

"Of course you do," replied Trevor. "But they don't determine success. Different people use different systems and techniques, successfully or otherwise. So it's not the system. It's your focus. Look, success in futures trading is a function of good decision-making. Now, if your focus is on whether you have enough money to trade, or whether you've got all the information and opinions you believe you need to have, or whether the market is settled enough, or which technical indicators are the most reliable, well, then you're going to make bad decisions. Just like you told me you hit a bad shot in golf when you were in your swing circle. For myself, I'm more focused on my target. My attention is on what I want to achieve. I concentrate on that. Then I read my reports and look at my charts and I make a decision; and I tend to make good decisions. You see, the same as you learned to trust your natural ability in golf today, I trust mine in futures trading. I assume that I can trade successfully, and somehow I do. But I'll tell you right now, it's not because I have any advantage over anyone else in terms of ability or inside information or circumstances. I create my success."

Trevor didn't have the apologetic look on his face he had had when he began. Now he stood there and spoke with a casual self-assurance I'd never encountered in anyone before. There was no hint that he was pushing his pet theory or even proving some worldview. He was simply stating something he knew in the bottom of his heart.

Those last words, "I create my success," hung in the air for a moment, and then Trevor said, "That's the trick, Mark, that's the trick. And it applies to everything in life. When you go from focusing on the process to the end result, you shift from the mechanical nature of the universe to the magical, as you've witnessed today."

Trevor didn't say any more. He knew he had made his point. Kaye and I both stared off into space absorbing what he had said. What was dawning on me was how addicted I was to process, or the swing circle, as Steve had called it. While Steve had disabused me of the notion that I had to concentrate on my swing, I had still believed there were processes vital to futures trading — until Trevor unburdened me of those. What other swing circles was I automatically stuck in? I shuddered to think.

At this point, Kaye suddenly asked, "Are you guys hungry? All these cocktails and no food. Why don't we go around the corner and get a bite to eat?"

Taking our leave took us close to an hour. By the time we were at the door, the last of the other guests were leaving too, and our host, Cliff, headed off with Trevor, Kaye, and me to eat at a Chinese restaurant opposite his terrace.

When we got to the restaurant it was fairly late, and they let us in only because Cliff was a good customer. We took our seats in a private room at the back, and the proprietor himself handed us our menus with a fanfare that acknowledged Cliff as a highly valued patron. My heart sank at the size of the menu. It was about twelve pages long and listed some three hundred dishes. Out of the corner of my eye, I saw Trevor open his menu at a random page and then snap it shut and put it aside as if he wasn't interested. Cliff and Kaye studied a few sections of their menus and then put them down and began chatting about people at the party they hadn't seen for ages. I sat there squirming over the vast variety of choice. When the maître d' came back for our order, I couldn't remember even a single dish, let alone choose one. Trevor looked up and asked for the Peking duck wrapped in pancakes. Kaye and Cliff ordered a selection of dishes to share. I was still turning the pages of the menu lamely. "Try the Peking duck and pancakes," Trevor urged me.

Even though they were having something else, both Kaye and Cliff said, "Oh yes, the duck and pancake is to die for."

Inspired by their enthusiastic recommendation, my sense of frustration lifted and I happily gave my order. I breathed a sigh of relief and smiled around at the others. "You've obviously had the duck before?" I remarked to Trevor, less for assurance than to make conversation.

"Never eaten here before," he shrugged.

"Then how come you made your choice so quickly and recommended it to me?" I asked in astonishment.

"That's how I make my decisions, Mark. I'll probably have to kill you, because now you've discovered my trading secret." He winked at the other two.

"You just made a random decision?" I asked, still taken aback by his impulsiveness.

"Not a random decision," replied Trevor. "It was a very deliberate decision."

"What do you mean?" I knew Trevor wasn't making fun of me, but I failed to see how his menu selection had been anything other than impetuous.

"Well," he said, "it's like making a trade. I know what I want: a great meal. That was my conscious intention when I walked in here. My mouth is watering from that intention. Then — what's the owner's name, Cliff?"

"Mr. Lai," said Cliff.

"And then," continued Trevor, "Mr. Lai brings us the menus, and I have to make a choice that is going to decide whether I have a great meal or not. There are two ways I can do that. I can read through the 315 menu items and compare them all to each other and everything I know about Chinese food from my past experience — even though that experience might not be relevant to this restaurant — and then make an assumption about what will most satisfy me. Or I can just rely on my natural ability and open the menu blindly, cast my eye over the page, and select the dish that, for whatever reason, stands out. If you can hit a great golf shot with your eyes closed, why can't I pick a great meal the same way?"

Trevor looked at me and then chuckled. "Of course, you might hate the duck. Often people lose money on my trading advice."

"So the trick is to trust your own ability?" I mused.

"The trick," said Trevor emphatically, "is to take your focus off the process and put it on the end result. Of course, if you don't trust your natural ability you'll be stuck in the process — like you were, agonizing over the menu."

My professional curiosity was piqued. "So the fundamental information you subscribe to, all the technical analysis, the timing and cycle data, do you actually bother to look at it?"

"Thoroughly," replied Trevor without hesitation. "Word for word, every statistic, every conclusion, every bit of information."

"Why bother?"

"For two reasons. First, some of the data is the raw material for my trading system. Second, I don't assume I know anything. I'm totally open to having factors or formations interpreted for me. The important thing, though, is that, while it's part of my process, I don't rely on it. I rely on my own natural ability."

I looked at Kaye and Cliff. Far from being left out of our two-way conversation, they were both listening intently, nodding and mumbling their approval at what Trevor was conveying to me. "You know what's strange?" mused Trevor. "People pay me for advice and lose money following it. How can that be, when I make money following my own advice?"

The others left the answer to me. "Because they don't trust themselves. That keeps them in their swing circle, as it were. They're focused on their ability and circumstances, not their target."

"Exactly, " said Trevor with a good-natured smile. He held his hand out for me to shake. Just then a couple of waiters arrived with our order. Mr. Lai hovered behind them making sure everything was in order. Trevor called out to him, "Mr. Lai."

Mr. Lai came forward. "Yes, sir?"

"Mr. Lai, I have a rather strange request. I hope you don't mind."

"Sir?" said Mr. Lai, allowing himself an indulgent smile that broadcast the fact that he'd be surprised if any request could shock him.

"I'd like a raw potato and four drinking straws."

"A potato and four straws!" Mr. Lai's eyes opened wide with puzzlement. He looked at Cliff to judge whether his friend was making fun of him.

"Please," said Trevor, "I want to show this young man a trick."

"Ah, a trick." Mr. Lai laughed with relief. He looked around at each of us in turn, nodding his head in comprehension. "A trick. A trick," he muttered to himself as he walked away from our table.

Mr. Lai came back with a potato and four straws on a tray. He placed the tray on the table and then stepped discreetly to the back of the room to observe what use a potato and four straws could be put to. Trevor held us in suspense as he chewed deliberately on a mouthful of duck and then slowly wiped the corner of his mouth with his napkin. He took a sip of water and coughed theatrically. "Okay," he said. "This is the object of the exercise: We have one straw each. Whoever can push their straw through the potato doesn't have to pay for their meal. Whoever can't do it pays. I'll go last. Who wants to go first?"

Cliff, known for being gung ho, instantly plucked the potato off the tray and picked up one of the straws. He looked quizzically back and forth from the potato to the straw, acknowledging the futility of the objective with a wry smile. He held the straw like you would a screwdriver and proceeded to try to screw the straw into the potato. The straw managed only to pierce the skin before it crumpled up like a concertina. Cliff put the potato and his mangled straw back on the tray with an air of satisfaction, as if he had just proved a point to everyone.

I wanted to get my own farcical attempt over with as quickly as possible. I grabbed the potato in my left hand and clutched the straw like a dagger in my right. I imagined that if I brought the straw down with enough force it might stab into the potato. I wasn't very confident. I felt like a fool for even attempting something so impossible. In my mind, the potato became a rock and the straw a flimsy tube made of powder — I could picture the straw crumbling to dust as it struck the potato. I stabbed violently at the potato. What I'd imagined would happen happened. I wouldn't have believed it possible, but my straw was compressed to about half its original length. My effort, however, had only slightly nicked the surface of the potato.

Kaye had a sly look on her face, as if we were playing cards and the time for her to play her ace had arrived. "I know the answer," she said triumphantly. "You boil the potato for half an hour. That's it, isn't it?"

"Of course!" cried Cliff, slapping his forehead.

"Nice try," laughed Trevor. "Very lateral of you, Kaye. But we haven't got half an hour. The objective is to put a straw through a raw potato."

"Can I make a hole in the potato with something else first?" asked Kaye, her voice and body language taking on a prickly edge.

"No," said Trevor, "just the straw and the potato."

"Well, go on. Show us how it's done, then," said Kaye.

Trevor put down his chopsticks and picked up the potato and one of the remaining fresh straws. "Now, Mr. Lai," he said, beginning to ham it up, "you've never met me before, have you?"

"Never before," Mr. Lai confirmed.

"This is not a trick potato, is it?"

Mr. Lai chuckled. He was getting the joke. "No trick."

Trevor held the straw and potato exactly as I had done. He looked at the potato casually for a full minute, then closed his eyes. In one even motion he brought the straw up and plunged it down into the potato. It seemed like the gentlest of actions, but when he held the potato up, the straw was sticking right through it.

Mr. Lai gave a startled cry in Chinese. After a few seconds of silence, he cried out again. Some moments later, curious faces began peeping through the doorway of our private dining room. Mr. Lai spoke rapidly in a combination of English and Chinese. He kept pumping his fist up and down and pointing to the speared potato. His staff looked at him impassively. Frustrated at not making an impression on them, Mr. Lai angrily barked out something in Chinese, and one of the faces disappeared from view. Not much time had passed before the same face reappeared at the door and two hands extended into the room holding out a fresh potato and a clutch of straws.

"What's this?" laughed Trevor.

Mr. Lai took the potato and straws from his waiter and pressed them on Trevor. "You show trick again," he importuned. "They ask to see trick for themself."

Trevor sat unmoved. "I'll do it if they try it first."

After a few instructions from Mr. Lai, the restaurant staff came into the room one at a time to have a go. Their efforts were met with the unbridled hilarity of their colleagues. When the last one had tried and failed, she handed the potato back to Trevor and laughed good-naturedly. "If you can do this, you must be able to walk through walls," she told him. The others looked at Trevor, their faces bright with anticipation.

Trevor contemplated the potato for what seemed like ages before he held it out to me. "Here," he said. "Why don't you show them how to do it?"

My heart skipped a few beats. I was surprised at my own performance anxiety. I thought of what good sports the restaurant staff had been about having a go, while here I was afraid of being derided for not having the power to perform the trick. Perhaps if I hadn't boasted to Trevor earlier about how I'd discovered the key to bending reality to my liking, I might not have been so bashful. I took the potato from him, as if compelled by an invisible force I was powerless to resist.

I looked down at it hopelessly, my face clouding with embarrassment. All I could imagine in my mind was the straw crumpling up. The potato became a rock in my hand; the straw, a fragile stem. With every moment that passed, the task became more and more impossible. My face began to flush with resentment at being forced to demonstrate my own incapability.

"Just remember," said Trevor, "it's a trick of the mind."

My first instinct was to tell him to shove the potato somewhere it could sprout, but that impulse was immediately suppressed by a flash of inspiration. "Of course," I thought, "I can do it." Trevor had just given me the secret to his trick. It was a trick of the mind. And the trick was to go from thinking about *how* I could stick a straw through the potato to thinking about the end result of the straw *going through* the potato.

Just that simple realization changed my whole demeanor instantly. I wasn't someone aligned against everyone else in the room, caught up in a life-or-death struggle to prevent myself from being seen as an idiot; I was just one of the team having fun with a crazy experiment. Something Steve had said more than once in our lesson came back to me: Remember, the game isn't about hitting a good shot; it's about imagining yourself hitting a good shot. If you stop trying to hit good shots and begin imagining good shots, you'll start hitting good shots.

My attitude changed from one of desperation to one of lighthearted fun. I really didn't expect the straw to go through the potato, but I'd give it a go anyway. I closed my eyes and pictured the straw going through the potato like a knife going through melted butter. I opened my eyes again and looked at the potato, imagining the straw sticking through it. I just kept looking at the potato and imagining that end result. Without my thinking about it, my right arm lifted automatically and plunged the straw into the potato.

When you hit a really good golf shot, you don't actually feel like you've hit anything. In a sense, you feel nothing — you're empty. All except for a sweet, ringing sensation that vibrates through your body. That's how it felt when I stabbed the straw through the potato: just an emptiness in me that resonated with an exquisite sensation I'll never be able to describe in words.

The room erupted in pandemonium. The waiters and

cooks lost their reserve and rushed in, shouting and laughing over one another. Mr. Lai forced his way through to me, shoving and barking, and lifted the potato out of my hand as if he were claiming the whole accomplishment for himself. Acting as though I didn't exist, he held the speared potato up in the air and began impressing on his employees how they were all witnesses to the impossible.

Down at sitting level, Trevor was enjoying the evidence of his magical premise. He didn't utter a word, but the beaming smile on his face said it all. A look of comprehension was dawning on Kaye's face. "Of course," she said, shaking her head incredulously, "it's the focus. It's always the focus."

"It's always the focus," agreed Trevor, laughing. "Come on, don't look so miffed. The potato and straw gets everyone. Hardly anyone believes a straw can go through a potato. It goes to show how insidious our assumptions are, how easily they divert our attention from the end result."

"So, the reality is," said Cliff, "a straw will go through a potato. Anyone can stick a straw through a bloody potato, can't they?"

"Sure," said Trevor with a look of even greater satisfaction. "Anyone can use their focus to stick a straw through a potato when they're told the trick. But can they use that secret to live their life?"

I felt too high to be drawn into the friendly bickering. I took another bite of my duck wrapped in pancake. Even before I'd speared the potato, I'd already decided it was one of the best meals I'd ever tasted.

INTO THE LION'S DEN

Thus began my initiation into the fantastic world of magic. I lay in bed that night quivering with the excitement of a child the night before Christmas. It was as though I were a blind person given the gift of sight. Golf was a mirror of how I'd been living my life: I'd assumed it was full of impossible rules that had to be learned and then mastered with unswerving dedication, application, and effort. All my life had been a tightrope walk, with me heading toward my objectives while juggling and balancing the impossible odds of success. One slip and I was gone. Now I had been opened to the possibility that life was a walk in the park.

Not that I was under any grand illusion. Trevor's words still rang in my ear. It was one thing to use the secret of magic to perform tricks, and quite another to live your life by it. While I had been initiated, I was well aware that I was no graduate. From what I could gather, both Trevor and Steve had been practicing their art for quite some time now and were continually learning and developing their mastery. Nevertheless, I'd seen enough to be convinced that there were two approaches to life. One full of effort that worked harder against the forces of nature the harder you tried, and one effortless, engaging the forces of nature the more you let go.

It took my breath away to think that the magic I'd believed in as a child was real. There truly was a force that, if engaged, could conspire with the universe to support me in bringing my dreams into reality. It wasn't just me and what I knew and what I could do while up against whatever life could throw at me. I didn't have to be like a gladiator fighting in the circus just to survive another day. I could be a free spirit at play in an enchanted world where everything came together naturally to nurture and protect me.

The timing of my introduction to this alternative paradigm was impeccable. The old gladiator was tired, and the lions were closing in. It occurred to me that the situation Kirsten and I were in must have been obvious to all our friends and family but even more so to our friends versed in the secret of living life for fun and profit. Talk about creating poverty and misery. I must have looked like the poster boy for the unfortunate 98 percent. As mortified as I was to realize how pathetic I must have appeared to Cliff, Kaye, and the rest of my intimate friends, I was nevertheless extremely grateful that they cared enough to set me up with such a dazzling exhibition of the principles of magic.

My time with Steve and Trevor had swept away everything I'd assumed about how the game of life had to be played. I wasn't sure exactly how to play it now, but I knew I could learn to play it in such a way that I could have fun and end up with everything I wanted. I had found my teachers and would do anything necessary to master the game. I would have my dream not because my circumstances would permit it but because I would know how to create it. That's what I fantasized, anyway.

Trevor had invited me to have lunch with him in town the following day. It was an unusual suggestion, because he didn't work in the city; he worked from home in the suburbs. But there was a particular restaurant he seemed to think would be most conducive to furthering our relationship. The plan was for me to pick him up at his house and drive him into town. We would have lunch and then go our separate ways — I to my business appointments and he to call on his trading associates.

Trevor and I had hit it off well on our first meeting. I found him to be a man of tremendous clarity, wisdom, and decisiveness — qualities I was all the more impressed with because of the humility with which he held them. Whatever Trevor saw in me, I knew that one of the things he appreciated about me was the eagerness with which I accepted his ideas about life. He could sense that he had found someone potentially as passionate about magic as he was.

Trevor climbed into the car and slapped me boisterously on the back. He was more like a kid heading out on a big adventure with his dad than some world-weary adult bracing himself for the grind of the inner city. He told me exactly where the restaurant was and the best route to get there. I asked him if there was a public parking lot within close proximity to our destination.

"Parking lot?" He looked at me sideways with mock incredulity. "Parking lot? What sort of creator are you, boy?"

"Where do you expect me to park?" I returned.

"On the street, right outside the restaurant," replied Trevor flatly. "That's the first thing you learn when you start creating. You create a parking space wherever you're going — at the front door."

"What, you just imagine it?"

"That's right, you decide it when you leave home. You imagine it, then you choose it, then you find it. Let's do it, because I don't want to waste my time walking around town."

Driving along the deserted suburban streets, I let my mind wander into the city and imagined myself parking in front of the restaurant. When we reached town and I turned onto the street the restaurant was on, I was dismayed to see NO PARKING signs all the way down the street. Sign after sign read LOADING ZONE ONLY — TOW AWAY AREA. Not for the first time, I felt silly for being sucked into one of Trevor's mind games. "How can you wish for something that isn't possible?" I thought to myself, feeling that Trevor had set me up to look stupid.

My annoyance was soon exacerbated by the fact that we became stuck behind a bottleneck of trucks maneuvering in and out of impossible parking spaces. A couple of workmen stood before the tangle of machinery, willing the traffic back with outstretched hands. Every now and then one of them would look back at the twisting hulks and shake his head at the improbability of the mess being sorted out. I sat there seething with frustration. Trevor was snapping his fingers and rocking his head to a tune on the radio. Suddenly he cried out with an alarm usually reserved for imminent head-on collisions: "Quick! Turn into this alley. Come on, man, wake up! The alley down here. There's a car leaving."

As I scraped past the bumper of the truck in front of us and turned into the alley, Trevor began whooping, "You did it! You're a genius! We're in. And it's right outside the club. Yahoo!" He punched me playfully a couple of times on the arm and called me a few unmentionable names that clearly were a sign of great respect and affection.

It was only a parking space, but I was shocked that we had actually found one. And not only was it a parking space; it was an unrestricted parking space — there wasn't even a meter. I didn't know such a thing still existed in the city.

"Just a relic of the past," said Trevor. "Don't worry, it won't be here the next time you come back."

Four or five steps across the narrow alleyway, and we were at the back entrance of the restaurant. Trevor stood under the faded awning that proclaimed "The Bull Market" in an old English font, one of his arms stretched across the doorway, blocking my way. "Hang on, didn't I say outside the *front* door?" He laughed. "Get it right next time, okay?" Then he opened the door and waved me through.

Even if I hadn't been dazed by my good fortune at having found a parking space, walking into the Bull Market would still have been one of the most disorienting experiences I had had in a long time. The cacophony that assaulted our ears as we descended into the cellar-like premises sounded like that of a thousand men in a dungeon cheering a boxing match. Down below was a huge subterranean hall packed with tables. Crammed around every table were ruddy-faced men dressed in dark suits and dazzling ties, with the occasional female, also in business attire, sandwiched in among them. All around the hall, huge television monitors mounted on the walls silently broadcast live sporting highlights from around the world, the commentary summed up in text at the bottom of each screen.

In stark contrast to the bellowing men around them, stunning women wearing nothing but gold lamé hot pants and suspenders floated demurely through the sea of suits, holding platters of roast meat and frothy tankards of beer above their heads.

It's not often that I feel intimidated in a restaurant, but I have to admit that my knees were practically knocking together even before I had taken the last steps down into the garishly lit dungeon. It reminded me of how I had felt back in Africa every time I'd been forced to track a wounded beast into the jungle — like something was going to come flying at my throat out of nowhere. While the whole scene was cloaked in a veneer of respectability, the atmosphere itself was tinged with menace.

As we hit the bottom landing, a man who looked like a retired heavyweight boxer crashed his way through the throng of patrons waiting hopefully for a table. His brusque familiarity with everyone in the queue marked him as the proprietor. Dressed in a suit calculated to be smart but not outdo the flashy outfits sported by his clientele, the big man stopped in front of us and, without giving me a second glance, embraced Trevor enthusiastically. "Mr. Campbell, what an honor, sir!" he said, beaming. He stood back and held Trevor by the shoulders. "Always a pleasure to have the world champion grace our humble establishment. How are the pork bellies treating you today?" While he spoke with a mock reverence, there was no mistaking the true affection in his voice.

Trevor proved equally adept at glad-handing. He grinned back at the proprietor. "Stavros, you big stud!" he laughed. "Good to see you, too, you old dog! Of course, when it comes to wine, women, and food I defer to you — you're the king." Raising his voice, Trevor shouted to the assembled company, "He's the king. He's the king." He raised both hands in the air like pistols and pointed his fingers down at the big man. A few people cheered. All of them laughed.

The compliment hit its mark. Stavros shook his head with undisguised pleasure, a bashful smile creasing his craggy face. Out of deference to his famous patron, he finally turned to me and introduced himself. "A friend of the great maestro?" he inquired.

"Business partners," answered Trevor on my behalf. "This is Mark Vale. He's my information man."

"Information," Stavros raised his eyebrows in a gesture that suggested he had deeply miscalculated me. "Well, that's the name of the game, isn't it?" His face relaxed into an expression of exaggerated sincerity. "Anything we can do for you," he said. "Anywhere, anytime. You're the information man." He grabbed two menus off the reception counter and blazed a trail for us through the crowded hall. We followed him up to a mezzanine level above one side of the hall, where the tables were spread out more spaciously and we could hear each other without having to scream. Stavros seated us at a table for four and snapped his fingers. A gorgeous waitress stepped forward and graced us with a radiant smile. "Jilly," said Stavros solemnly, "these are my friends Trevor and Mark. Take away these extra places and give these guys special treatment. First round of drinks is on me." To us, he said, "Gentlemen, enjoy," and took his leave. He hadn't taken two steps from our table before I heard his voice boom, "Mr. Wallace, sir! What an honor to have the greatest business mind in the city grace our humble establishment. If the queen doesn't give you a knighthood this year, I'm going to fix her myself."

Trevor waited for the laughter at the next table to subside. "So," he said, "what do you think?" He stretched out his arms as if to say, "Amazing, isn't it?" Jilly, too, looked at me with radiant expectation.

I looked down at the chaotic scene below us. I didn't know what I thought, much less what to say. All I knew was that I felt decidedly uncomfortable. Looking up at Jilly's angelic face and quivering breasts did nothing to help my uneasy state. I felt an unwelcome stirring in my loins and a hot flush on my face. My brain was turning to soup, bombarded as it was by a barrage of mixed messages. All I could do was gape, like a fish trying to breathe out of water.

Unfazed by my embarrassment, Trevor took it upon himself to order for both of us. He spoke to Jilly casually, not seeming to notice her bare flesh heaving in his face. After he had ordered our food, Jilly asked him what we'd like to drink. "Just water," replied Trevor. Even though I was desperate for a stiff drink, I felt too weak to protest.

Once Jilly had taken off, Trevor turned to me with a sympathetic smile and said, "Can I tell you what you're thinking?"

"Here we go," I thought, but I said, "Sure."

"You're thinking, 'What the hell are we doing in a place like this? Why did he bring me here? It's a noisy hole in the ground full of alcohol-soaked wankers leering at half-naked women. Why aren't we in some chic little bistro with the rest of civilized society, where we can talk happily without being confronted by overt male lust and aggression? What are we doing a century back in time in a nouveau riche playpen that exploits both women and the basest nature of men?' How am I doing so far?"

"Pretty good," I admitted with genuine admiration. While I was mortified to have my private thoughts exposed, it was also good to have someone clarify them for me. And the absence of judgment in Trevor's voice made it easier for me to bear.

"Before we go on, though," said Trevor defensively, "let's get something clear. You do want me to teach you, don't you?"

"Teach me?" I spluttered.

"Yes, teach you. Isn't that why we're together? You want me to teach you magic — how to apply the trick of the mind to living your life."

Trevor's words sparked something in me. I felt a pang of excitement shoulder its way through the heaviness inside me. There had been no discussion between us about Trevor taking me on as a protégé, but now that he'd named our relationship I felt I'd better seal it before he changed his mind. "For sure!" I blurted out, too keenly for my own liking.

"Good." He smiled disarmingly. "So now, then, aren't you always angry with me the moment before something magical happens?"

I thought back to all the dark emotions that had boiled up moments before I'd stabbed the potato and just before we had found the parking space. It occurred to me that I'd also felt the same anger and frustration not long before Steve had me clipping golf balls through the fork of a tree with my eyes closed. I looked down to avoid Trevor's eyes and nodded my head sheepishly.

"That's okay," Trevor reassured me. "In fact, it's great. You know why? Because it teaches you the first secret of magic."

"Which is?" I said, brightening up again.

"Well, you tell me. If you're feeling bad one moment, and then the next moment you attain something beyond your own belief, what does that tell you?"

I searched my mind for the meaning behind the dynamic Trevor was referring to. Nothing occurred to me. I shrugged.

"The first secret of magic," said Trevor dramatically, "is that your thoughts and feelings aren't real." He sat back to let the profoundness of his statement sink in.

"Not real!" I groaned in dismay. "Don't tell me that. I've invested too much in my thoughts and feelings for them to not be real. I've been working on my thoughts and feelings for years. Isn't that the whole New Age thing — to honor your feelings?"

"Look, it's important to acknowledge your thoughts and feelings," said Trevor. "Soon you'll find out why. But the fact is that your thoughts and feelings don't express reality; they express your assumptions."

"What do you mean?" I frowned. Having my theories about golf or market speculation shattered was one thing; having my entire reality trashed in a single statement was something else altogether — something I wasn't at all prepared for.

"Well," said Trevor, holding my attention with a forceful tone of voice, "why do you think you're experiencing those negative emotions as you attempt to do the allegedly impossible? It's because you assume it can't be done, that you're not going to get what you want. So you feel anger, frustration, resentment, despondency, depression, fear. Those feelings are just telling you what you believe. Emotions are nothing more than the spokespersons of your belief system.

"I mean," he went on, "what happens the moment you do the impossible, or realize its possibility? You feel good, don't you? When you hit that great shot, or the traffic flows for you, or you find the parking space, you suddenly assume you can have what you want in life. When you assume you're connected to what you love — what you're going for — you feel positive. When you assume you're separate, you feel negative. But as you know from playing golf, and driving in traffic, and pushing a straw through a potato, and scoring a parking space where you wanted one downtown, your feelings don't know what's really going on or what's really possible. Magicians never identify with their thoughts and feelings."

"So what do you have to go on?"

"Your heart. What you love. The end result you want," Trevor sang out. Lowering his voice again, he said, "Which brings us back to what we're doing in this madhouse. First, let me say I love this place. The food here is on a par with the best in the city; the steaks are the best in the country, as you'll see. And, let's face it, it's the sexiest restaurant in town. Where else can you see so many gorgeous women without their clothes on? The first rule of being a magician is: Never deny your own nature.

"Second, if I'm going to teach you anything, how am I going to teach you in your comfort zone? How am I going to teach you to apply the trick of the mind to your life when we're in some safe haven that conforms to your sense of limitation? No, buddy, this snake pit is a mirror of your own consciousness. Every fear you have in your mind you'll find right here; every possibility in your life exists right here, too."

Trevor's point was punctuated by a huge roar from the

crowd. We both turned instinctively to the nearest television monitor. A bloodied boxer lay on the canvas like a murder victim; his crazed opponent, still not satisfied the fight was over, was being held back by a frantic referee.

Jilly arrived at our table to deliver our water and salads. "Main course won't be long now," she said, smiling. "Everything okay?" She stood with one hand on her hip, the other holding her tray, her chest pushed out provocatively.

Her presence literally took my breath away. I had to gasp for air.

Trevor hardly took any notice of her. "Fine, thanks," he muttered, waiting to launch back into his lecture.

"Thank you," she said, flashing us another mesmerizing smile, and left us to our business.

Trevor didn't miss a beat. "You see," he continued, "you have a twenty-four-hour experience of creating whatever you want. You learn that all you have to do is focus on the end result and you can achieve anything. You play great golf, you bend the traffic to your will, you push a straw through a potato, you create a parking space outside a restaurant in an area of no-parking zones. You're on a high. You feel like a god. Then life happens — you walk in here — and you go to pieces. How come?"

I didn't think he wanted an answer. I just shrugged.

"Because your assumptions take over, that's why. You walk into this place, and what is it? It's a testosterone factory. It's a pleasure dome for urban heroes. There's the best food in town, topless goddesses, alcohol, real live titans clashing on the big screens. It's not much to look at from the outside, I know, but when you come down those stairs you've walked into the winners' circle. These are the self-styled masters of the universe. This is where the champions enjoy the spoils of war. You're up to your armpits in the most ambitious men the city has to offer, men primed by these surroundings to reach their most intense level of competitiveness.

"You stumble into this den of masculine aggression, and you assume you have to compete with these guys. You assume you have to compete with them on their level. Furthermore, you assume you don't have what it takes. You're not rich enough, successful enough, suave enough to compete for the gorgeous waitresses. You're not aggressive enough, quick enough, accomplished enough to handle the mind games. You're physically threatened. Most of these guys would love to prove themselves in a fight. You're afraid of being torn apart. You don't believe you're viable in here. You assume the conditions aren't right."

Trevor was on a roll now, and I was right there with him.

"At the top of the stairs, you're the man who can hit any target. By the time you reach the bottom of the stairs, you're in your swing circle. You've totally lost your focus. You don't even remember that you wanted something — that you came here with an end result in mind. I had to remind you that you wanted to learn something from me; I had to order for you. What do you think has happened to you?"

I didn't know the answer to that one either, but for once I didn't mind my ignorance being exposed for what it was, along with my defective focus. I knew I was absorbing the most important lesson of my life.

When Trevor saw that I had no answer, he opened his eyes wide and spoke in a weird voice, "You're losing your mind, man." Then he broke into a smile and punched me playfully on the arm. "I'll tell you what happened," he said, his voice becoming grave once again. "You come in here and your assumptions hit you. Your assumptions hit you in the form of thoughts and feelings, which you take to be objective reality. Because you feel them and think them, you assume that the conditions you perceive, and the limitations you perceive, are real. So you automatically begin coping with them. All your power goes into your circumstances.

"All your conditioning has trained you to resolve your thoughts and feelings, which in turn are insisting you deal with your circumstances. Your thoughts and feelings trap you in the process, in the swing circle. Emotional stability becomes the name of the game. You think that if you feel good, and feel powerful, and feel safe, and feel loved, then everything will flow from that. It's like thinking a good golf shot will follow your getting everything in the swing circle right.

"But I'll tell you right now, a magician doesn't think that emotional stability is the name of the game. A magician knows that thoughts and feelings are the siren call that leads you away from what you want. I mean, think about it: how did you feel about golf before you met Steve Addington?"

"Frustrated, hopeless," I said.

"And what did you do about it?"

"Well, I gave it up."

"And that made you feel better?"

"Yup. The pain went away."

"And how did you feel about walking in here?"

"Mmmhhh..." I snorted. Trevor had put me on the spot with that one. Nevertheless, I resolved to be as honest as I could. "Intimidated, daunted, overwhelmed."

"Afraid," Trevor offered.

"Afraid," I nodded.

"Small, insignificant."

That was harder to admit to, but I did.

"So, how would you normally have resolved all those feelings?" asked Trevor.

"With a stiff drink," I laughed, happy to introduce a touch of levity to our intense discussion.

"I bet," chuckled Trevor. "But before you even sat down? Before you even reached the bottom of the stairs?"

"To be honest," I said, "I wouldn't come to a place like this. I'd just leave."

"There it is," cried Trevor, making me start as he hit the table with his fist. "There it is," he said again. "You leave. You give up. That's how you resolve your negative thoughts and feelings. And because you feel better after you give up, you walk around believing you're okay. You play games that don't challenge you, and you gravitate to bland environments, and you do business with clients who aren't threatening. You do things the safe, easy way. You park in commercial parking lots and take your lunches in trendy little cafés that are about as exciting as libraries. And you think that because you don't feel overly bad, you have defeated the things you reject. You imagine that your nonparticipation is actually a form of power. But you don't see how cut off you are from the flow of life. You don't know that you are drying up inside. And sooner or later, this will reflect in your day-to-day reality."

I didn't think anyone had ever spoken to me so bluntly before. What made it easy to swallow was that, again, there wasn't a shred of judgment in Trevor's voice. Even though I could relate personally to what he said, the way he spoke gave me the impression he was talking about human nature generally, not about me specifically. Rather than feel insulted or admonished, I received what Trevor said as a gift.

After taking a sip of water, he carried on. "Negative thoughts and feelings create a tension that begs for resolution. Everyone has their favorite way of resolving that tension. Some tend to fight, some tend to submit, and people like you prefer to retreat. We all use all of these strategies some of the time, but we tend to favor one of them." He made a broad sweeping gesture that included the whole hall. "Here you'd feel especially uncomfortable, because, as a runner, you're surrounded by fighters. But the point is, no matter what you do, whether you fight, submit, or flee, you've always got your attention in the wrong place. You're stuck in how you believe you have to be, and you're doing what you believe you have to do.

"It goes back to trust. You don't trust your own nature to take care of you, to work things out in your favor. So you try to force it, to do what you believe will guarantee your viability. When you're stuck there in the process, stuck in the swing circle, you're separate from the end result and separate from the natural ability that can create it for you. You believe that you can't naturally have what you want. Your thoughts and feelings are merely expressions of that assumption. And your reactions to your thoughts and feelings are your attempt to compensate for your beliefs."

Trevor smiled at me weakly. It was his way of apologizing for burdening me with so much information. There was no need, though. I was rapt in what he was saying. As he spoke I could see two paths in my mind: one that appeared very attractive in the beginning — broad and paved and sunny — but that ultimately led into a swamp; another that appeared at first to be unappealing — dark and narrow and overgrown — but that actually led to an island in the sun. I remembered the story of the magician Assam, and there was no doubt in my mind which path the 98 percent followed and which path the 2 percent followed. Your choice of paths, I realized, determines whether you create poverty and misery or fun and profit.

What Trevor said next crystallized the insight developing in my mind. "Ultimately, there are two realities you can live in. One is the reality of your thoughts and feelings, where you are constantly compensating for the notion that you are separate from what you want and don't have the ability to naturally attract it to you. The other is the reality of your vision, where you are connected to the end result of what you love and are relying on your natural ability to make it happen.

"In the past twenty-four hours, every time you focused on an end result, you disproved your assumptions about the possibility and process of that undertaking. This demonstrates that your assumptions form an illusion. So on the one hand there is what you love, and on the other you have your illusion. The choice you have as a human being is to create what you love or perpetuate your illusion. What determines your experience in life is simply which reality you focus on."

Just as Steve had done on the golf course at one point, Trevor looked about us and, leaning closer to me, spoke in a strident whisper. "You see, that's the second secret of magic: Your focus creates your reality. You've probably heard this somewhere before, but do you know what it really means?"

"I do now," I assured him. What he was saying made a mockery of the whole way I'd been living. I now had a picture in my mind of pushing a wheelbarrow loaded with struggle, apathy, and defeatism down the path leading to the swamp. Yet in the light of what Trevor was saying, it didn't matter. The important thing was that I could see the other path now, and it was beginning to dawn on me how I could get on it. "If I just take the idea back to golf," I said, eager to demonstrate that I'd grasped the moral of the story, "it's like being frustrated and uptight because I'm afraid I don't truly have the ability to hit the ball properly. I struggle with forcing the ball to do what I want it to. I end up playing badly, and this ultimately makes me feel even worse. Alternatively, I could forget about what I think or how I feel and just put my energy into focusing on the target, not on how

I'm going to get the ball there. I would end up playing better, and as a result, I would feel better."

"That's it," said Trevor. "That's it. But it's also a matter of what you attempt in life. The less you limit yourself, the greater your experience of life. The joy of golf lies in hitting those sweet shots. If you assume you can't play well, and don't, there's a whole lot you're missing out on. The joy of life lies mainly outside of what you believe is possible. The whole point of magic is to defy your belief system and live your bliss.

"Living is like making love. Think about the sweetest sex you ever had. It was fresh. You were with a new woman or you made love in a way that was new. You don't have juicy sex when it is with the same partner in the same bed in the same position night after night. That's junk sex. That's junk life. Life is only great when it's new and fresh, when it's outside of what you have always known."

Something about Trevor's presence suddenly changed. He didn't formally close the subject, but he didn't have to. In an instant, his attention let go its grip on me and opened up to include the entire hall. It was a relief to be freed from the intensity of his focus. When Trevor looked back at me, he wasn't the same person. Gone was the earnest expression. Now there was a mischievous glint in his eyes. He had magically transformed from the studious tutor into a freshly arrived partygoer.

"Hey, let's have some fun," he said, with a carefree laugh that released the tension of his lecture. "Where's the food? I'm starving."

4 DISCOVERING THE HEART

I had no idea what Trevor meant by "Hey, let's have some fun," but the more I thought about it, the more uncomfortable those words made me. What was his idea of fun? Were we going to write off the rest of the day, carousing with the drunken rabble in the mosh pit below? If that was his plan, I had some important appointments with major clients that afternoon to think about. Besides, hanging around a bunch of loudmouthed yahoos competing for the attention of naked women wasn't my idea of fun. And if he meant trying to pick up the waitresses, that was against my principles. Never mind the fact that I was a married man; harassing someone in a position less powerful than my own didn't count as appropriate behavior in my book.

Trevor looked totally relaxed. He gazed about the hall with a slightly amused look on his face. Every now and then he would catch someone waving to him from the crowded floor. His response was always the same: a big warm smile and his right hand raised in what was either a peace sign or a victory sign. At one point, I could clearly hear his name being chanted above the din of the crowd. We both looked around to see where the chant was coming from. A whole table of young men had risen to their feet, and when they were satisfied Trevor was looking their way they began bowing in unison and crying out, "We're not worthy. We're not worthy." Trevor looked at me and laughed with deep pleasure. He got to his feet and bowed back at the group.

Seeing Trevor so at home in these surroundings only served to highlight how out of place I felt in the Bull Market. This was not my scene. These were not my people. The sooner we got out of here, the better. The only redeeming feature about the place was that it had served as the forum for Trevor to teach me the first two secrets of magic — that thoughts and feelings are illusions, and that your focus determines your reality. For that I was grateful.

I now believed that I could achieve anything I set my sights on. What troubled me, though, was how I habitually returned to my swing circle, blindly trying to figure out the situation or circumstance I was dealing with. I had seen the power of focusing on the end result, and I intellectually understood that it applied to everything in life. Yet when it came to discussing futures trading or stabbing a straw through a potato or creating a parking space in the city, I had involuntarily regressed to the process that I automatically assumed applied to those endeavors. Even when an experience had reinforced the integrity of focus, I was unable to apply that insight to the next situation. Only twelve hours before, I had been lying in bed dreaming that life was magically going to transform itself into whatever I wanted it to be. Now I was sitting in a basement full of people I thought were losers, feeling completely out of place. I didn't feel like the god who could create whatever reality he wanted; I felt like a worm — hopeless and helpless. Who was I kidding? As if I'd ever be a magician. I couldn't even hold my own in a crowd of snotty-nosed securities dealers.

And yet this was just what Trevor had shown me with the first secret of magic: that in every situation I faced, my thoughts and feelings would come up afresh to tell me that I couldn't trust my natural ability, that I'd have to rely on my acquired ability and seek out conditions that were more favorable. Because I'd been conditioned to assume that thoughts and feelings expressed reality, I was compelled to cope with the process rationally. My thoughts and feelings always frightened me out of focusing on the end result and out of relying on my natural ability.

Trevor was right. The bawdy restaurant was a mirror of all my beliefs. Here I was surrounded by a small army of corporate mercenaries fiercely polarized at the opposite end of the spectrum of values I held sacred, all of them fortified with the courage alcohol bestows. What chance did I have of fitting in, let alone having a good time?

And the topless waitresses, what power did they have? Probably the knowledge that the men were competing for their affection, and that they were on a pedestal beyond the reach of even the most ferocious competitor. What chance did a pacifist like me stand with women like these? Sitting in the Bull Market didn't make me feel good; it made me feel worthless and weak.

I could see clearly how my thoughts and feelings, as long as I identified with them, would sap me of the will to keep my end results in mind. What Trevor had said made me realize that in order to remain conscious of the target, I had to understand that thoughts and feelings didn't express reality, and thus I didn't have to automatically respond to them. That realization freed me from the spell of my swing circle. The power of the first secret of magic was that I could look at my thoughts and feelings to see what I was assuming in any given situation. And, with the awareness that assumptions were only assumptions, I could then put my focus back on the target.

Knowing that I had grasped a profound insight into the art of magic made me feel great. However, I didn't know how to apply it to the glum predicament I found myself in.

"Gee, the food's taking a long time," I said to Trevor.

"Of course," he replied. "That's the whole idea."

"What is?"

"To get you to drink. That's where they make their money. It's a brilliant system. You come in here, and the aggression and sexual tension make you uptight. You need to resolve your own inner tension. So you drink."

"Well," I said, "why don't we get with the system and have one ourselves?"

"Uh-uh," Trevor shook his head. "That will just weaken you. As soon as you resolve the tension, you're back in your swing circle. You think all these people here are at an advantage because having a drink has made them feel comfortable and sure about themselves. But in truth, they're at a disadvantage. They've given their will away. You might be sitting here feeling uncomfortable, but you haven't given your will away yet. You haven't resolved your tension yet."

"I'm not sure I'm with you," I said candidly.

"Okay," said Trevor, shifting in his seat as though he were preparing for a lengthy explanation. "The first secret of magic is that your thoughts and feelings aren't real. Your thoughts and feelings express your assumptions in any given situation. As such, they're designed to make you respond to what you're thinking and feeling. If your thoughts and feelings are limiting in any way, they will create a tension that intensifies until it's resolved. When you take action to resolve the tension, you might experience emotional relief, but you're back in your swing circle. Your focus has gone from your end result to coping with your assumptions. You're back doing all the things you believe you need to do in view of the fact that you can't trust your natural ability."

"Is this the third secret of magic?"

"No, it's a function of the second secret, that your focus creates your reality. You see, your discomfort is only intensifying because you're focusing on it. You're trying to work out what's causing it and how you can make it go away. You're feeding your assumptions, and they are growing more and more powerful. Your answer to your own inner tension is to get out of here as quickly as possible or to start drinking heavily."

"What's so wrong with that?"

"Nothing." For the first time ever, I noticed a look of irritation on Trevor's face. "You can leave or you can start drinking, and there's nothing inherently wrong with either of those options. It's just that if they're designed to resolve the tension, they are coping with your assumptions. And if you are coping with your assumptions, you are going to perpetuate them." He nodded his head toward the rowdy mob of suits. "What do you think those guys are going to create here today? Do you think they'll have learned anything, had any meaningful exchange? Do you think they'll go to bed with one of these waitresses? Do you think they'll do a good deal over lunch? Do you think they even appreciate the food they're eating? Most of them just feel good; they just feel powerful, being part of all this, being included in the winners' circle. But you look at them from the outside, and they're just clowns. That's how they're going to feel about themselves tomorrow. And then they're going to rush here at lunchtime again to resolve their tension by having naked goddesses act as if they fancy their idiotic behavior.

"You see, it's not that these people aren't men of high achievement; they are. It's just that when they come here they give their power away. At work they are ruthlessly focused on the bottom line, and they work ferociously toward that end. Here, though, they forget what it is they want and descend into behavior they hope will lead to acceptance, which they hope will lead to good things. Maybe they'll get seduced or promoted. Who knows? It's like the swing circle you refer to in golf: they're imagining that getting everything right in the swing circle will somehow translate into hitting the target."

"So what are you doing here?" I asked, partly out of genuine curiosity and partly out of anger at being subjected to the discomfort I was experiencing.

"First," Trevor said, in a voice that firmly held his own ground, "we're here to learn magic. I'm here to teach you the valuable art of applying the trick of the mind to practical living."

His words immediately made me feel ungrateful for the interest he was showing in me, but what he said next really made me feel ashamed of myself.

"Second, I'm here for a good time. I can create whatever I like here. This place holds every possibility imaginable for me. Just because you see personalities playing out here, don't think these aren't great people. These are my peers; many of them are my colleagues and friends. If you get to know them, you'll find they are brilliant, interesting, and fun in their own way."

I looked down at my lonely salad glumly and swallowed. I was beginning to feel miserable. If this was magic, would I ever be able to grasp it?

Trevor changed to a more conciliatory tone. "Feeling pretty lousy now, huh?"

His concern made me warm to him again. "You could say that," I said, smiling ruefully.

"Well, that's okay," Trevor reassured me, "because even though you feel lousy, you still haven't resolved the tension, and if you don't resolve the tension you can still create whatever you want from here."

The only thing I could think I wanted was to resolve the tension — to feel better, to have a drink, to go outside, escape. But I knew these weren't choices a magician was supposed to entertain. "So what do I want?" I asked in exasperation.

"You see, that's the question of someone who doesn't believe he can have what he wants," said Trevor matter-of-factly. "Everyone knows what they want; they just dismiss it because they don't believe they can have it."

"So what do I want?" I insisted.

"Well," smiled Trevor, pleased to see that the lesson was advancing once more, "there are several things you want. You want to learn about magic. If you just remembered that, you'd feel a whole lot better. You wouldn't mind your circumstances if you appreciated what you stood to gain here. But that's another matter. Something else you want is to make money. That's why you're in town, isn't it?"

The sound of the word *money* bucked me up a little. I nodded enthusiastically.

"You see, there are things you want. You want to have a good meal, you want to have a convivial lunch, you'd absolutely love to feel Jilly's breasts."

"What are you talking about?" I stammered, the hot flush on my face siding with Trevor's assertion.

"Hey, it's okay," said Trevor. "Remember the first rule of being a magician: Never deny your nature. Even if you aren't going to act on it, you should always allow yourself to know what you want. The only real choice you have in life is between what you think and feel and what you truly want.

"Right now, as you sit there, you want to learn about magic; you want to make money; you want to have a good meal, feel at ease, and enjoy good company; and you want to jump on one of the naked bodies torturing your eyes." Trevor held up a hand to stop me protesting. "But you're in conflict. You're a married man. The beauty of these women intimidates you. You're in hostile territory. You can't see how you can have what you want. What you want threatens you. It brings up all your assumptions about how you are not viable. You experience this as an unbearable tension inside you.

"The easiest way to resolve that tension is to deny what you want — to forget about it, let go of it. Which leaves you with your thoughts and feelings. Then you think that your thoughts and feelings express what you want. As if what you want is to run away from here and hide, or start drinking heavily.

"Remember the second secret of magic is that your focus creates your reality. If you give away what really matters to you, your focus is by default going to go to your thoughts and feelings. That just leaves you in the reality of what you fear. The counterbalance to the tension of your thoughts and feelings, to your fear, is what you truly want, what you love.

"To be able to create by magic, you need to be able to hang out with two things: what you want, and the assumptions you have about getting and having what you want. The first thing you need to do is take the power out of your thoughts and feelings. You need to acknowledge them. Until you observe them objectively, they will be controlling you; you will be acting on them automatically. If you want to turn this whole experience around, that is what you will do right now. Just notice your thoughts and feelings, notice what you are assuming, what you're telling yourself right here and now."

I would have given anything to turn this experience around. I eagerly examined my own thoughts and feelings. Upon closer reflection they were more or less what I'd seen already. They were a mixture of anger, resentment, apprehension, and shame. They implied that I wasn't powerful enough to cope with my surroundings, that I wasn't man enough, and that I was bad for being here, that it was somehow depraved to enjoy the decadence of the place I was in.

Far from being a painful exercise, however, confronting my own perceptions turned out to be uplifting. There was suddenly a separation between myself and what I thought and felt. I could see my beliefs quite dispassionately. They were not me, but rather like a forgotten script inside me — an antiquated tape full of absurd notions. It was as if the original, powerful part of me that had been banished took over my consciousness again. I sat there and surveyed the scene quite calmly. I could still feel a few qualms coming up, but overall I didn't feel as threatened as I had before. I was less affected by the chaos around me. It didn't have anything to do with me. I suddenly felt I knew where Trevor's aura of equanimity came from.

Seeing the change in me, Trevor went on: "There, you see how quickly you can take the power out of your thoughts and feelings? The next step, though, is a little more difficult, but only because you're not used to it. What you want to do now is fully acknowledge what you love — this means what you really want, what truly matters to you. Love is the power of magic. Without it you are nothing. You have to let yourself dream. You have to dare to admit what is there in your heart."

I tried opening my mind to what I wanted. It was as though I could sense something over my mental horizon, but every time my attention began heading in that direction, an intense uneasiness would summon it back to the blank part of my consciousness. I could have rattled off the list of things Trevor told me I wanted, but that wouldn't have come from any conviction within me. Hard as I tried, I couldn't go past simply wanting to feel better than I currently did. The answer to that objective, while not as urgent as before, remained the same: run away!

Trevor soon sensed my block. "You can do it," he urged. "You just have to remember that most human beings are stuck between their fear and desire. You're afraid you don't have what it takes to have certain things, whereas with other things you're afraid that you actually can have them. You're afraid that your inadequacies will keep you separate from what you want, and that if you were in touch with your power, it would destroy what you already have. Like in here, for instance, your assumption that you're not good enough for these women makes you feel small."

Something in his tone and the piercing look he gave me made it clear that, in no uncertain terms, Trevor could see that the attitude of moral indignation I had assumed in the Bull Market covered for a deeper sense of personal inferiority. As benign as his signal was, the realization of how transparent I was to someone who had known me for such a short time still made me feel as if ice were running through my veins.

"But more unnerving than that," he continued, "is your terror of what would happen if you were good enough. What would happen if you could go home with one of these babes? What would happen if you could satisfy your every desire? What would happen to all the structures in your life, all those conditions you have established and agreements you have made? Where would that leave you and your family? You and your wife? You and your friends? You and your clients? You and the people who depend on you? You and the people you depend on? What if they could all satisfy every desire of theirs? It's like opening a can of worms, isn't it?

"You see, you don't even realize it, but you've made a contract with the rest of society to not be powerful. Hell, there'd be chaos if everyone had whatever they wanted. That's what we believe, anyway. So we enter into an unspoken agreement that we won't rock the boat. We won't do anything that frightens anyone else. And we expect others to keep to the agreement, too. Anything we do that frightens anyone else is bad, and anything anyone else does that frightens us is bad.

"Your powerlessness is just a reaction to your power. Your swing circle is just a place in which you pass the time when you're not allowing yourself to be powerful. When you deny yourself your own power, all you're left with is your manipulation and control.

"But, you see, it's all based on the mistrust of your natural ability. Virtually everything we do in life, or the way we do it, is based on the mistrust of human nature. You don't trust that what you desire is good for you and everyone else. You believe that we are all separate, that what you want is in conflict with what others want. But how can you say you're alive if you're in a little corner with everything toned down to its blandest, with everything reduced to its common denominator?"

Trevor seemed to want an answer. How would I know? I was crouched in my little corner. I could feel how small it was. I shrugged apathetically.

"Well," he went on, "we know that if you focus on a target you'll hit it. But what if you hit a target and, by so doing, destroy a bigger target? What if you slept with Jilly? What would you lose by doing that? That's the big fear, you see. That you might lose something more valuable. And what's the most valuable target we have?"

I gave another shrug.

"Approval. Validation. Love. Belonging." Trevor was leaning into me again. He had me bound in his focus once more. "Everything we do, we do in order to have those things or to be impervious to their absence. In the game of life your swing circle is ultimately focused on ensuring that bigger target of love and belonging, which you unconsciously believe your survival depends on. So you are not going to trust your own nature with that one. You're going to control it.

"That's why people can do simple tricks like hitting a golf ball with their eyes closed or putting a straw through a potato but can't apply the related principles to living their lives, because it means relying on their own natures, on their natural abilities. And everyone's afraid of where that would lead."

"So what's the way out of that?" I heard myself ask.

"Bring the principles to the bigger target, of course," said Trevor, as if the answer were the most obvious thing in the world. "Focus on your highest good. Focus on what will ultimately serve you and everyone else. And then let your natural ability do the rest.

"As above, so below. The principle remains the same at every level. Your natural ability can be — no, must be — trusted at every level of endeavor. If you want to live the greatest life imaginable, you're going to have to begin trusting yourself, you're going to have to let your nature do what it wants to, as wrong and as scary as that might seem at times."

A whole lot of ideas and images tumbled into my mind, one after the other, as soon as Trevor stopped talking. The first was a memory of how awkward I felt when I was hitting golf balls with my eyes closed, and yet how sweetly I struck them anyway. Next came a vision of all the different levels of endeavor in my life and a sense of how they were all the same thing, differing only in how high I perceived the stakes to be. And crowding in behind that came the realization of what I wanted.

The notion that my natural ability could take care of everything on every level had the most profoundly liberating effect on me. As Trevor had talked, I had felt a growing annoyance at my need to protect myself from the consequences of my own passion. Enthused as I was about the full extent of my innate power, I shrugged off my feeling of uneasiness and, taking my self-consciousness by the scruff of the neck, marched it over the forbidden horizon of my own psyche. The unexpectedly pleasant state of mind I found myself in made me gasp, like one does when plunging into a cold swimming hole on a hot summer's day.

It was as if I had stepped outside the swing circle of my own consciousness. I felt as though I'd fallen out of my head and dropped into my heart. The place where my consciousness was now resting was void, not of awareness or feeling but certainly of any strident mental or emotional activity. I could sense that happening somewhere above me, though I felt remote from it and unaffected by it.

As I experienced life from this newfound perspective, I realized I'd never really seen the world firsthand before. I had been like a blind man groping around in the dark, relying on an argumentative committee of thoughts and emotions for guidance and direction. From this fresh perspective, my view was not overladen with notions of what everything meant and deliberations of what to do about it all. Everything was allowed to live in peace. And in that still, unhurried space, what truly needed to come to my attention came into sharp relief in its own time. My world became dazzlingly clear.

This clarity was accompanied by a thrilling sensation I have since come to understand as joy. It is the emotion that surfaces at the prospect of living immediately face-to-face with life, as opposed to the drudgery of constantly having to cope with the circumstances we believe we are subject to. The first thing I realized I wanted was this feeling, though it was more a state of mind than a feeling. When Trevor said I wanted to learn magic, he was in a sense right, but I now appreciated that what I really wanted was what magic could give me. And this was it. More important than being able to accomplish impossible feats and acquire any possession I desired, I wanted time out of mind. I wanted to be free of the drama going on in my head; I wanted to step outside my illusion and be up close and personal with life; I wanted to embrace reality, know life just as it was.

With my newfound clarity I looked about the hall, and what struck me was the mass of humanity right before my eyes. I saw a mob of human beings not very different from myself, all unconsciously striving to get back to their hearts, all groping around for their joy with their thoughts and feelings. The second thing I realized I wanted was to be connected to all these anonymous people. I wanted to share my awareness and enthusiasm for life with them and let them share with me whatever they felt they had to give. An almost tearful emotion surged through me as I opened myself to the qualities of humility and respect. These were qualities I greatly admired in Trevor, and I was touched to find them in myself.

Up on the mezzanine floor, Jilly and a stunning Eurasian woman whose name was Karen were waiting on the tables around us. Although there was nothing obvious on the outside that would prove it, I couldn't help but feel they were both really enjoying themselves. I felt there was something about staying on top of the overwhelming workload itself and having to deal with the crude attentions of the hoards of men that gave them a deep satisfaction. They were like surfers riding an impossible wave, and the thrill of it was that they hadn't fallen off. One moment they were in a flap over some mix-up of orders, and the next they were laughing good-naturedly at some risqué remark made for their benefit. Whatever was going on, they could handle it, and it was that accomplishment that gave them their juice.

Seeing them now from my unclouded, unconfused state of mind — or was it nonmind? — I was able to fully appreciate both Jilly's and Karen's exquisite beauty and withstand the awesomeness of their sexuality. But it was something I could appreciate without having to conquer or own. That part of me was just an old idea of how men were supposed to respond to women. What I truly appreciated now about Jilly and Karen was their greatness of spirit — their capacity to generate positive energy in what must have been extremely tough conditions. It was this aspect of them that I wanted to connect with and relate to.

Now that I was in touch with what I really wanted, I could appreciate the truth of what Trevor had said: that my true nature would never want something that wasn't good for everyone. The power of love, I could see, was that what

I wanted opposed nothing else in life. In my heart I sought no power over anyone else; I did not aim to take anything from anyone that they weren't happy to give. I wasn't some thief. Even in relation to my agenda of being in town to make money, I had something valuable to exchange. What I truly wanted would give as much as I took. It was easy to go for. My struggle was all in what I thought I had to achieve.

The sense of relief I felt inside must have been palpable to Trevor. He grinned with the same satisfaction Steve had shown once I'd started letting go of my golf swing. "There you go," he laughed. "Welcome to the land of plenty."

"The land of plenty?" I inquired vaguely. Most of my attention was still on observing my newfound state of well-being. Part of me was suspicious that it would disappear as quickly as it had appeared.

"Yes," said Trevor, "the land of plenty. That's the world where everything you want exists. That's the world you want to live in."

"As opposed to . . . ?"

"The world where everything you want doesn't exist."

"What are you saying?" I shook my head in an effort to give Trevor my full attention.

"Well, just that your focus creates your reality. When you focus on the end result of what you want, you realize that you have it already. Your emotional experience is higher. The process of taking what you want is effortless. Look at you." Trevor nodded at me almost accusingly. "A moment ago, you were dying to jump on Jilly. You were all torn up about that. You hated yourself for wanting her, and you hated yourself for not doing something about it. Now you see her humanity, and all you want to do is connect with it. That's easy. That's possible. The thought of that lifts your spirits."

"How do you know what you know?" I asked in amazement.

"Same as you," replied Trevor. "When you're outside your thoughts and feelings, you know. When you're outside the swing circle, you're guided by your natural ability. You look around at everyone now, and you know their thoughts and feelings. You know what's really going on all the time. You just have to trust your natural ability." He leaned over to me and said in the most confidential murmur, "That's how I trade the markets. I read all the signs physically, but that's just to stimulate my knowing. My natural ability is connected to the markets. It knows. And I just trust that knowing."

I hardly heard a word he said. "It's just amazing," I said, my attention still on the emotional transformation I had just experienced, "the difference in me since I stopped to observe my own thoughts and feelings and then allowed myself to know what I really want. I feel like another person entirely. I'm even happy to be here. And I haven't taken a single step toward what I want. Before I've even created anything, I feel like I already have what I want. Because it's this state of mind I want. It's just amazing." I shook my head and let myself feel the elation.

Trevor gave me a moment to enjoy my high before he

spoke again. "Well, now you've discovered the third secret of magic," he said softly, "and I'd say the most important secret."

"Which is?"

"That everyone has a heart! You have a heart. This is a big one. You can't practice magic until you understand this secret. Everything hinges on what you've come to now."

I knew that I felt good and that I could see everything clearly, but I didn't know what Trevor meant by "everyone has a heart." I asked him to explain.

"Sure," he nodded. "You probably understand that I'm not talking about your physical heart that keeps your blood pumping. Nor am I talking about your innate decency, goodness, or compassion, or the warm, fuzzy feelings you may have, although they're all related to your heart. What I'm talking about is that you have a pure nature that seeks to participate in the wonder of life. You have a nature that not only is creative and expressive but that also feeds off the creativity of the universe. Your nature lives by breathing creativity in and out, in and out.

"Having a heart means you have an essential nature and that, furthermore, you want to express and experience that nature. You want to indulge that nature. That's your passion. You want to live from your own inner spark and connect with and enjoy the spark in others. That's the whole point of the human race. Even if 98 percent of the population doesn't get it.

"It's a powerful realization, though, because what your heart wants is very easy to get. It's simple. Look at what you really want. What is it? To appreciate life, to appreciate other human beings? Well, you've got that already. To make money? You've got that, too. You've got your appointments. Turn up at the meetings, and a percentage of people will buy your products. How easy is that? When you know the absolute bottom line of what you want, it's easy to have.

"You see, the struggle comes from not knowing your heart, not knowing what you truly want. And people don't know what they truly want, because they're stuck in what they believe they have to do to get it."

"What do you mean?" Trevor had lost me in the last two sentences.

"What does everyone want? Huh?" he asked, and before I could even think about the question he answered it for himself. "They want their hearts. Just like you, they want to stand in their hearts and know their truth and make their lives about that. That is their bliss. But why can't they do that?"

"Because . . ." I began, actually feeling confident of the answer.

"Yes, that's right," Trevor cut me off, "because they don't trust their own natural ability to support them in having it. They don't trust what they naturally know and what they naturally do. So they fall back on what they have learned to want and how they have learned to behave.

"Let's take you, for example." I could feel Trevor's focus boring into me now. "You walk in here, and what do you think?"

This time he seemed to want an answer, but by the time I opened my mouth he was talking again.

"That's right, you see this as a war zone. You don't see the humanity here. You don't see the end result as connecting with human beings; you see the end result as surviving them. You imagine having to take on a hall full of savage strangers. That illusory task overwhelms you. It causes you psychological pain. Being here in that frame of mind is really difficult.

"And the women? How do you react to them? You're not in your heart, so you don't see them for who they are. You see them as symbols of power. You have to have them in some way, even if it is just to have them hold you in high esteem. So then you have to build up your power. You have to be more than you are.

"I mean," Trevor allowed himself a good chuckle, "this place is your ego's worst nightmare. You are competing with guys who earn a million bucks a year, posers in suits that cost as much as your car, guys who represented their country at the Olympics, former sports heroes, guys with helicopters, guys with yachts. I mean, you know that every day these gorgeous women are being propositioned with holidays in the south of France and weekends on tropical islands; they are having gold and diamonds dangled in their faces. Man, you'll have to do some impressive crap if you're going to join in that game — which you will when you don't believe you can be real and still have what you want."

I let out a sigh of relief. Thank God I wasn't on that futile path right now.

"See what I mean, now?" said Trevor with a knowing look.

"Sure do," I replied. I thought Trevor would leave the point there, but he wasn't done yet.

"And then, when you leave here, you will go to your appointments, and if you're not in your heart you'll forget that you're providing a service. You will see your clients as people who are trying to stop you from getting what you want. From that standpoint, you'll work on overpowering them, outsmarting them, tricking them, seducing them, befriending them, looking for their sympathy. Then, at some level, they will feel manipulated and they'll resist you, so you'll have to try harder. You'll unwittingly talk yourself out of more sales than you could get."

Trevor now allowed himself a big sigh, as if the thought of all that effort had worn him out. "I tell you, it's a struggle. All these people," he waved vaguely about the hall again, "they're all struggling. Even old Digby Wallace, Esquire, the billionaire.

"You have to understand that people can achieve things outside of magic. People still play good golf while concentrating on their swing, don't they? But the point is, no matter what they achieve, they've done it the hard way. They have struggled against the flow. And after all that struggle, they don't even end up with what they want. They end up with lots of what they believe they need to have or be. They may be rich or highly educated or full of theories or sly or have the perfect image, but do they have their hearts?

"Your heart is the path of least resistance. If you know your heart, life will always be rich and life will always be easy. That's why you must always ask yourself, is this a path with heart? Is this mood my heart? Is this course of action my heart? Is this outcome my heart? If you ask yourself that in all your affairs, then you're going to go a long way; you'll be living life for fun and profit."

As if to prove the power of his magic, our main courses finally arrived at the moment Trevor concluded his lecture. I looked at my watch. We had been waiting for over half an hour. Not that I minded. In that time, Trevor had taken me through a psychological transformation I never would have believed possible. While the positive frame of mind I was in would have been enough for me, I could also imagine that so much more of what I wanted could flow from that frame of mind. I felt something I hadn't felt for a long time — I was excited about life.

Jilly announced her arrival with a big "There we are!" and a commensurate smile that advertised how proud she was to have organized our meals so speedily. She laid down the plates of juicy steaks smothered in a creamy prawn sauce before us and took a step back. "Pepper?" she inquired brightly, holding up a pepper grinder as if it were a prize on a quiz show.

Trevor and I both said yes at the same time. Jilly stepped toward the table again and leaned over it slightly to crack the pepper onto our steaks. No matter that I was back in my heart, the sight of her spectacular breasts inches away from my face gave me goose bumps. I didn't know whether it was just nerves, but I burst out laughing.

"What's the matter?" she asked nervously. Trevor, too, looked at me in consternation.

"I'm sorry," I said once I'd recovered my composure, "it's just that I've never been in a situation like this before. I mean, this amazing food served by someone as stunning as you — half naked! For a moment there, I thought I was dreaming. It's like a dream, you know. I wanted to touch you to see if you were real."

"Oh, that's okay," said Jilly, smiling sympathetically. "It is a bit weird, all this." She rolled her eyes around. Then she stuck out her arm playfully. "You can touch me, if you like." She glanced at her own breasts meaningfully. "It's all real," she added.

There was something so easy and genuine about this woman that moved me to say, "I'm sure you are, and extremely beautiful at that. But you know what really impresses me about you is the grace with which you float around here. You stay so positive and give everyone such positive energy — it's an inspiration. That's more beautiful than anything." I was surprised at how freely and intimately I was able to speak to someone whose beauty and sensuality scared me so.

Jilly let her whole body shiver with pleasure. "Oh, thank you," she sang. Turning to Trevor, she said, "You can bring him back anytime. He's obviously not a futures trader."

"Yeah, yeah, yeah." Trevor held up his hand to stop her going any further. "Put your hot pants back on, baby. You know he's married? I just brought him here so he could remember that there's still life on earth."

Jilly looked at me as if she were a Jewish mother

slighted by an ungrateful son. "You know what you get when you cross a pig with a futures trader?" she asked.

"No, what?" I chuckled.

"Nothing. There are some things pigs just won't do." She laughed, ruffling Trevor's shock of black hair affectionately. I laughed with her.

"That's with a lawyer," protested Trevor. "That's a lawyer joke, idiots."

The incongruity of the world champion being at a disadvantage made us laugh all the harder. "Yeah, yeah, yeah," grumbled Trevor with mock gruffness. "Haven't you got work to do, smart ass?"

Jilly left us to our food, flicking Trevor with her table towel as she strutted off. I sat there savoring my meal. As Trevor had prophesied, it was the best steak I'd eaten in my life. I marveled at how, only a few minutes before, I'd been so uncomfortable you'd have thought I was about to face a firing squad, and now here I was enjoying the finest food in town and having a laugh with a naked goddess. That was a turnaround that could only be ascribed to magic.

Trevor looked at me while he chewed. He swallowed and said, "You know, that was a really nice thing you said to Jilly. If you keep on coming from your heart like that, you won't even recognize your life by tonight."

5 TAKING ACTION WITHOUT DOING ANYTHING

Trevor and I ate our lunch pretty much in silence, both of us savoring the mouth-watering food and soaking up the atmosphere of the rowdy beer hall. At a table on the floor beneath us, an equal number of men and women — a rare sight in the Bull Market — occupied themselves with jovial conversation. One or another of them was constantly pointing out something going on in the hall, then all the others would crane their necks to see what that person was talking about, and then someone would make a crack and they'd all laugh till some of the women had to wipe tears from their eyes. One of the women called her waitress back, and she must have asked about a ring the waitress was wearing, because the latter held out her hand for the whole table to admire. Everyone stretched over for a closer look. One of the men made a comment, and everyone, including the waitress, laughed uproariously. When the laughter had died down, the waitress held out her hand again and began recounting some anecdote, which she concluded by holding the back of her hand to her forehead in mock despair, her whole body shaking with mirth. Everyone doubled over with laughter again, a few of them slapping the table for relief.

At one of the tables beside us, a group of men drew our attention to the oversized television screens with loud groans of vicarious pain. The channel was showing highlights of football tackling fouls. A big, beefy player was brought down by two high-tackling opponents, and a third jumped on his groin. One of the men looked away with a weeping look on his face, silently mouthing a string of profanities. He caught my eye and grinned.

"Ouch!" I empathized.

"He'll never be a baritone again," my neighbor grimaced. From then on, he began including me in his witty observations, and it felt good to be reached out to like that. I was enjoying our facetious connection.

The irony of how I now felt about being in the Bull Market was clear to me. It was incredible, I thought, that I could have such ill feelings about a place and then, in the next moment, enjoy its vibrancy and want to be part of the action. It seemed to me, from the remarkable series of examples I'd experienced over the previous twenty-four hours, that life was divided into two worlds: one where everything you loved was possible, and another where you were blind to that potential. In the former, you sat back and enjoyed the fruits of possibility, and in the latter, you stumbled around cursing and blaming and making excuses, doing what you could to deal with your separation from that possibility. It seemed to me that magic was the ability to cross over from the empty-handed world to the abundant world. It was just a trick of the mind. It depended on whether you chose to believe in your assumptions about what was possible or chose to believe in what you loved.

I looked at Trevor and considered him for a moment. It occurred to me that as much as I liked and admired him, most of the time I had been under his wing I had been angry and resentful toward him. And yet, even though he hardly knew me from a bar of soap, he had graciously borne that hostility all the way along the path of transformation he had taken me on. Not once had he stooped down to the level of my fear and negativity. The whole time, he had stood steadfastly anchored in his world of possibility, waiting patiently for me to cross the border between my narrow world and his. I was moved by a deep sense of gratitude toward this virtual stranger who had taken it upon himself to guide me back into the light.

As we were scraping up the last morsels of food on our plates, I said to him, "You know, Trevor, I really appreciate your teaching me this stuff. You couldn't have taught me any better." I laughed at my earlier resistance to everything I had gone through with him.

Trevor dismissed my thanks with a wave of his hand. "Hey, man, I'm just where I would be anyway. It's no big deal. You ought to thank yourself. You're the one who created the lesson for yourself." He saw me thinking about that one. "Yeah, that's right," he stressed. "You create it all.

Don't think you create only the things you consciously go for. Everything that's happening in your life is a result of where your attention is, on some level or other. All credit to you, man." He saluted me with his glass of water. "You know, you wanted to learn about magic, so you went for that, and along the way your stuff came up — you got scared and shitty and whatever — but you didn't resolve the tension. By not resolving the tension you kept your natural ability in play. And look where you landed, buddy. You couldn't have hit a better shot on the golf course, could you?"

"No," I agreed, "but I couldn't have done it without you."

"Well, I did keep you focused," Trevor acknowledged. "But, hey," he spread his arms out, "what are friends for?"

I held my glass up in a toast to him. Then I thought back to the principles he had taught me. "So those three secrets you talked about, are there any more?" I asked Trevor.

"Absolutely," he answered. "I expect there are more secrets than I know about; but even the ones I know about, I can't teach you all of them."

"Why not?"

"Because, while I can practice them, I don't embody them all," said Trevor enigmatically. "Only an old person can tell you about being old, and some of the secrets you'd have to learn from a woman."

For a moment, I thought he was being smutty, but his straight face told me he was serious. I felt deflated knowing that Trevor had no more to teach me. I was beginning to enjoy the cathartic process of his instruction. "So there's nothing else I need to know? No other secret?" I asked a little peevishly.

"Well, I suppose there's no harm in telling you the fourth secret of magic now," said Trevor.

"What's that?"

"The fourth secret of magic is that there is never anything to do, but always action to take." He spoke in a tone that signaled he didn't expect to be taken seriously.

"What does that mean?" I asked.

"Well, I suppose it's something that has to be demonstrated. We'll wait till Jilly comes back to clear the table, and maybe she'll help us." Trevor showed no inclination to say anything more about the subject. He looked up at the big screen. "What do you think of Brazil's chances in the game tonight?" he asked offhandedly.

Jilly wasn't long in coming around to our table. "Finished here?" she chimed. "How was that, gentlemen?"

"That was terrible," said Trevor with a poker face, pointing to his empty plate. "Take it back and bring me another one." Jilly wrinkled her nose up at him and gave a few little piggy snorts.

"Actually," Trevor's voice became serious, "there is something you can help us with."

"Oh, really?" said Jilly suspiciously.

"Yes. Can you sit on Mark's lap so I can take a photo as a souvenir of his visit here?" asked Trevor bluntly.

Jilly gave Trevor a "you've got to be kidding" look, and Trevor looked back at her impassively. It seemed as if the whole hall had gone silent. A blind rush of panic froze me in my seat. What kind of creep would Jilly think I was? I imagined Trevor and me being kicked and punched by the crowd as the big, broken-nosed Stavros dragged us out of his tavern, ejecting us for our disgraceful conduct.

But then Jilly's face brightened. "Why not?" she shrugged. "Come on, you, let me in."

"I didn't say anything about . . . I didn't . . ." I stammered.

"Of course it wasn't your idea," cooed Jilly condescendingly. "Now, are you going to let me in or not?"

Trevor had already whipped a Polaroid camera out of his bag. He motioned with his hand for me to move my chair back, which I did mechanically.

"Come on, don't be so stiff," giggled Jilly. "That's it." A flash went off and Jilly squealed with surprise, then she gave me a tight squeeze and stood up again. Trevor pulled the photo out of the camera and set it on the table.

Jilly stood beside Trevor with a hand on his shoulder, watching the picture develop. At first, her expression was clouded, but as the picture began emerging, she started laughing, and then laughed harder and harder. By the time the picture was fully developed, Trevor too was laughing hysterically. When his laughter had calmed down to a spasmodic sighing and sobbing, he pushed the photo across the table for me to have a look at. It showed Jilly snuggled up to me with her arms wrapped tightly around me. Her right breast was flattened against the left side of my jaw and her right leg was kicked out high in a theatrical gesture. All you could see of me was two startled eyes that looked as though a proctologist had just inserted his finger in me. Even I had to laugh.

Everyone's good humor helped to wash away my embarrassment. If anything, I felt mildly giddy from the lingering sensation of Jilly's flesh and the intoxicating scent of her perfume still toying with my olfactory senses. The man who had run the facetious commentary on the football fouls asked to see the photo. I handed it to him, and he showed it to his luncheon companions. Rather than find it so amusing, they seemed to be impressed. One of the guys held the photo up and looked at it wistfully. "It's not every day a naked babe sits on your lap," he lamented.

"What about me?" another of them cried. "Can I have a picture, too?"

"In your dreams, boys," said Jilly haughtily as she walked off with our empty plates.

"There you go," said Trevor to me. "She doesn't sit on just anyone's lap." And then, as if the idea were coming to him on the spur of the moment, he said, "Why don't you ask her for a photo of her sitting on my lap?"

Trevor's suggestion caught me off guard. It wasn't something I was comfortable doing. It felt like a creepy thing to do — getting a naked woman to give someone else a thrill by sitting on his lap.

I thought of the best excuse to give Trevor for not doing it.

"You think it's creepy, don't you?" he said, reading my mind again.

"Yeah," I confessed, "and it would seem so disingenuous now, after me. It'd just be dumb."

"Well, that depends, doesn't it?" Trevor came back. "I

mean, it could be just fun. We all had fun when she sat on your lap, didn't we?"

All I managed to say was, "Mmmh...ugh...I...ah..."

"You're afraid of what other people will read into your intentions. I mean, isn't it cool having a photo of yourself with a Bull Market babe sitting on your lap? It's like standing at the pyramids or the Eiffel Tower. Come on!"

"I suppose," I conceded hesitantly. I could actually see his point.

"So there isn't anything wrong with it, is there?" cried Trevor. "Judgment is just the mind's way of masking fear." He wagged his finger at me. "Fear hides behind judgment. If you go back to your heart, you won't find any judgment there."

"Okay, okay," I shouted back at him in annoyance. "I'll do it, I'll do it."

What could the harm be? We had a good rapport. I would appeal to the power of Jilly's positive spirit. In my mind, I could see her responding cheerfully to my request.

Jilly was soon back at our table with the dessert menus. Her bright, engaging smile filled me with confidence. I was just about to open my mouth when there was a tittering from the next table, and the wag who had previously asked Jilly if she would take a picture with him piped up, "Hey, come on, Jilly. Why don't you sit on my lap, and we'll talk about the first thing that comes up?"

Jilly's face turned to stone, and she glared at the offending patron for what seemed like an eternity. There were a few supporting cracks from the man's friends, but they quickly wilted under the force of Jilly's steely gaze. In an icy voice that relegated them to a station in life somewhere beneath common garden slugs, Jilly hissed through gritted teeth, "God, you men are disgusting. Why don't you go to the toilets, and get it off your chest?"

Jilly turned back to Trevor and me with one of those "the things I have to put up with" looks on her face. "See anything you like, gentlemen?" she asked in a subdued tone.

Jilly's stinging rebuke of the men next to us had totally taken the wind out of my sails. There was no way I was going to be lumped in the same sleazy boat with them. Any resolve I had had was gone. "I don't suppose there's any chance of you posing for a photo on Trevor's lap, is there?" I said, making my request sound like a joke I didn't expect her to take seriously. "I didn't think so," I muttered as she shot me a "Don't you start" glance.

Trevor and I selected a dessert each, and Jilly left without favoring us with her bright good-bye smile. "Those idiots," I complained to Trevor, "they wrecked any chance I had."

"Nonsense," replied Trevor coolly, "you wrecked it all by yourself."

"What do you mean?" I protested. "Are you saying I created those guys' jerk-like behavior?"

"No," said Trevor, "they did that all by themselves. But Jilly not sitting on my lap had nothing to do with them. That was entirely due to your focus."

"But you saw how pissed off she was with them," I objected. "How could I ask her after they'd pissed her off like that? You saw the look she gave me. It just wasn't the right time. You asked her when she was in a good mood."

Trevor looked back at me impassively. "Have you ever heard of Gurdjieff?" he asked.

"Who?"

"Gurdjieff. He was a mystic who lived in Russia during the revolution. At that time, the town he lived in was surrounded by five different armies. Every other day, the town was overrun by a different army. Each new army went from door to door conscripting the boys and men, raping the women and girls, looting, shooting, killing. But every time they came to Gurdjieff's door — where, by the way, 132 men, women, and children sheltered — he would meet them at the door himself and ask them to go away, and they did! Imagine that.

"If you were caught collaborating with any other side you were shot. If you were caught with a firearm you were shot. Yet Gurdjieff openly carried a revolver wherever he went. He carried a permit signed and sealed by all five generals of the competing armies. What's more, he survived that siege, as did every man, woman, and child under his protection. Not only did they survive the siege, they even carried out an archaeological expedition sponsored by the opposing armies."

Trevor allowed a puzzled look to appear on his face. "What do you think his secret was?"

I could only frown in response.

"It was the fourth secret of magic," said Trevor. "What Gurdjieff said, and I quote, was, 'In every human being resides a heart, and I have learned that if I talk to someone's heart from my heart, then they will give me everything I ask for.' That's the fourth secret of magic."

I was confused. "Isn't that the third secret — that everyone has a heart?"

"Nope!" Trevor shook his head. "The third secret of magic is that everyone has a heart, but what Gurdjieff said goes further than that. You see, your heart is what you want, and when you communicate what you want, you create a bridge to having it. Most people communicate what they believe they need to do in order to have what they want, rather than communicating what they actually want. There is a vital distinction."

"Give me an example," I said.

"Well, that's easy," replied Trevor. "Let's use the example of you trying to get Jilly to sit on my lap. What you wanted was for Jilly to pose for a photo sitting on my lap. But what did you communicate?"

"That it wasn't important," I said after some thought.

"That's a good point," remarked Trevor, as though that hadn't occurred to him yet. "But you see, the thing is, Jilly was pissed off at the guys over there for asking her to do exactly what you were going to ask her to do. She was really angry, wasn't she? And you didn't want her to respond to you like she had to them. So what were you going for?"

"Not being cut down," I replied.

"Exactly," said Trevor, like a teacher congratulating his pet student. "So you made a joke of asking her. You communicated that you didn't expect her to sit on my lap, and even that you didn't expect that it was okay for you to ask or for her to actually do it."

"Yeah, but she had just blasted them," I argued. "How could I go and ask her straight out after she had just made it clear that she didn't want to know about it?"

"Well, that's between her and them," Trevor answered. "If someone hits a bad shot in golf, does that mean you can't hit a good shot?"

"I suppose not," I conceded. "But a golf ball is different. It hasn't got a mind of its own. It hasn't got a temper."

"So what you're saying, then, is that Jilly's mood has the power — other people's thoughts and feelings determine what's possible for you in life. If they feel good, you can have what you want. If they feel bad, you can't. It's the conditions, is it?"

"Well, people's moods affect outcomes. That's the reality, isn't it?"

"Ah, but is it?" cried Trevor. "You see, this is the very thing you need to understand to appreciate the fourth secret of magic.

"The fourth secret of magic says there is never anything to do, but there is always action to take. If you want Jilly to sit on my lap, the obvious action you have to take is to ask her to sit on my lap. Just like when you want a golf ball to go in the hole, you have to putt it. There's always action to take, and it's always obvious what that action is.

"But 'doing' is a whole other kettle of fish. 'Doing' is about fulfilling certain conditions you believe are necessary before you can get what you want. You believe that to get Jilly to do what you want, she's got to be in a good mood, she has to like you, and she has to be overtly happy about what you're asking her to do. So you then go about fulfilling those conditions. You don't do anything to threaten her; you don't ask for what you want directly. Instead, you make a joke and act as if what you want isn't important to you — you are afraid of owning it. That's 'doing.'"

"But you can't ignore her mood, can you?" I persisted.

"Well, that's what you believe," shrugged Trevor. "That's why you do what you do. But just look at the end result. The only thing to look at in life is whether you got what you wanted or not."

"I suppose I didn't get what I wanted," I murmured.

"No, of course you didn't," said Trevor forcefully. "It's just like golf, though, isn't it? In golf you don't trust your natural ability to hit the target, so you try to control the process. You take your attention from the target and put it on the swing. We don't trust our own nature to support us, see? Now, how do you suppose you're going to trust someone else's nature to give you what you want if you can't even trust your own nature? You can't, can you? So you're going to have to control that person.

"We're all very different in some ways." Trevor looked about the hall to include the whole spectrum of humanity in what he said. "We all use different strategies to control each other. We threaten, we cajole, we beg, we humor, we impress, we withdraw, we flatter — whatever we do, it's based on making sure the other person does what we want them to. No matter how passive our strategy is, the truth is, we don't let others do what we want; we try to force them.

"You see, you are in your swing circle looking at Jilly in her swing circle, thinking, 'How in the world am I going to get what I want here?' You are in your swing circle trying to control her swing circle. Can't you see how difficult that's going to be? Much easier if you just step out of the swing circle altogether and ask for what you want directly. That's what Gurdjieff was talking about: dealing with people outside the swing circle."

I shook my head in disbelief. I was amazed at how easily you could be deceived into assuming that the circumstances you currently faced were uniquely governed by something other than the law of focus. "So it always goes back to the end result?" I sighed.

"It's the focus!" exclaimed Trevor. "Nothing but the focus. If you don't get something in life, it's only because you weren't focused on it. There's no use making excuses, because that's all they are."

"So if I focus on what I want in life and communicate that, people will always do what I want?" I asked, still not totally convinced.

"Not necessarily," replied Trevor. "I mean, if you respect people's sovereignty, they may well choose to do something other than what you want. But being a magician isn't about getting your own way all the time. Being a magician is about creating what you love in life, and you don't have to have it your way all the time to have that. I don't even win the majority of the trades I make, but overall I still make a good profit.

"The point about dealing with people is that everyone has a heart. If you recognize that every single person has a natural ability to create the most fantastic outcomes in life, and you relate to that part of them rather than their petty nature, then your life will become an amazing experience. Overall, you'll end up having much more of what you want than you could ever have imagined possible."

Intellectually, I could understand what Trevor was saying. I just couldn't see how to apply it. "If I relate what you're saying to golf," I said to him, "I can totally follow you. With golf you just focus on the end result and swing. You don't worry about the swing, but that's the action you take; you swing. That's simple. There is only one option — the only thing to do is swing. How do you know what action to take in other endeavors where there are myriad different options, like when you're dealing with people?"

Trevor rolled his head vaguely from side to side, weighing how best to answer my question. "Well," he came back thoughtfully, "I guess you focus on the end result and then take action. What action you take is less important than your focus, because your focus will tend to influence your action.

"If you use the example of getting Jilly to sit on my lap, all that matters is that you're focused on the end result. From there, only one thing is obvious, isn't it?" Trevor raised his eyebrows as an invitation for me to respond.

"I have to communicate what I want," I said, decisively for a change.

"Yes," smiled Trevor. "You have to communicate what you want. But that's where the obvious ends. How you say it — whether you sound assertive or not, whether you're convincing or not, polite or not, confident or not — doesn't matter. It's like the swing in golf. It's the only obvious action to take, but whether your grip is right, and whether the swing feels good or not, doesn't matter. You may well get some things wrong, but other factors will compensate for that. Whatever you're creating, all you have to concentrate on is the end result, and then just do your best from there. Let all the forces at play do the work for you. That's why we say creating is effortless, because you don't have to control every detail; you just focus on the end result."

Trevor's face lit up as he hit on the subject closest to his heart. "I mean," he enthused, "it's just such a wonderfully free state of mind to exist in. It's the most relaxing, peaceful way of life you'll ever find. When you can trust your own creative nature to bring everything together, you can stop struggling and start living.

"But the trick in learning to trust is learning to allow failure." He smiled again, this time at the irony of his own words. "Most people see failure as proof that they can't trust their natural ability. They don't appreciate it as simply a function of focus. So rather than refocusing on what they want, they focus on not failing. Resistance to failure — when you say to yourself, 'I can't afford to fail' — will put you in your swing circle every time, because in your mind the only guarantee of success is control.

"If you can't fail, you can't achieve things by magic; you can't create," asserted Trevor in the tone of someone summing up the winning argument of a debate. "Because you won't be able to relax, you won't be able to focus on the true end result; you'll be in your swing circle."

My mind went back to when I'd allowed the possibility that the golf ball might not do what I wanted, and how that had freed me up to strongly envision the end result I was choosing. "So allowing that something might not happen isn't the same as giving up your focus?" I said, more in support of his argument than anything else.

"That's right," said Trevor, striking a more conversational note again. "It's not about wanting any less for something to happen; it's just about the meaning you put on things when they don't work out.

"If you are playing golf and you hit a lousy shot, there are two things you can tell yourself. Number one: I can't hit a golf ball. Number two: I hit a lousy shot. Number one will topple you into your swing circle. Number two will compel you to focus more diligently." Trevor shook his head as he spoke. "They're two different orientations entirely: One, an uptight approach where you're constantly struggling to get everything right, where you believe everything has to be perfect before you can succeed in life. The other, an easy, relaxed way where you know what you want and you just do the best you can."

"There's nothing to do, but always action to take," I mused, reflecting on everything Trevor had been saying.

"Yes," Trevor reiterated. "It's all about focusing on the end result and taking the action that most obviously has to be taken — any more than that is 'doing.'"

Trevor relaxed back into his chair, seemingly satisfied he'd conveyed everything there was to be conveyed on the subject. As for myself, I sat somewhere between inspiration and panic. On the one hand, I was emboldened by the intellectual reinforcement that my own focus was the sole determinant of whatever happened to me in life. On the other hand, I was panicked by the realization that Trevor and I both fully expected that I'd be testing out the efficacy of his premise by repropositioning Jilly. A nervous flutter went through my stomach as I heard her voice behind me.

"I'll just drop these desserts off and come back for that order, sir," she chimed in that sweet voice she had used with Trevor and me before the whole sitting-on-the-lap affair. Trevor signaled with his eyes that she was coming over to our table.

"Your desserts, gentlemen," said Jilly in what to my ears sounded like an icy tone of voice. She laid the pudding bowls down without any eye contact. Even her "thank you" sounded as if she was rebuking us for our ungracious behavior.

While my heart was pounding wildly at the prospect of being poorly judged by such a paragon of the opposite sex, a part of me cared only about whether I would make a stand for myself or not. It was more important to me to begin following through on what I wanted than to focus on whether I looked or felt good. And I knew I had a split second in which to act. Jilly wasn't going to be at our table any longer than that.

Maybe it was for the best that it all happened so fast, because otherwise I might've had time to dwell on my many misgivings. As it was, I didn't even look up at Jilly. I just looked over at Trevor and imagined Jilly perched on his lap. Almost at the same time, I found myself calling out, "Hey, Jilly, can you sit on Trevor's lap? I want to get a photo of you two together."

Even as I spoke I felt like a total idiot. I could hear my voice quavering, and I could imagine how pathetic I sounded to her, like some impudent peasant telling the Ice Queen what to do. But all the time I sat there cringing, I kept looking at Trevor and imagining Jilly laughing happily on his lap.

I was so flushed with embarrassment that my ears seemed to be blocked; I couldn't hear a sound. It felt as though a gigantic hush had fallen over the hall, as if the entire population were waiting with bated breath for Jilly's reaction. But the blow over the head with the tray or the cruel words I expected never came. Instead, my hearing came back in time to notice Jilly sighing with exaggerated annoyance.

"Gee," she scolded, actually sounding pleased at the persistent attention she was getting, "You guys never give up, do you?" Then, after a moment's consideration, she said, "I hope you realize you're asking me to do something a pig wouldn't do." The humor had come back into her voice. "But I will do it. I will do something not even a pig would do — on one condition!"

"What's that?" I asked, finally daring to look up at her.

"He has to take his clothes off, too."

"What?" cried Trevor indignantly.

"Well," said Jilly in the chirpy voice poker players use when they're holding a royal flush. "You're an arrogant bastard, aren't you? Sitting there like I'm some kind of plaything, you with your clothes on and me naked. Makes you feel safe, doesn't it?" Jilly stabbed Trevor in the chest a few times with her finger. "Well, what I'm saying is, let's level the playing field. Then I'll be happy to pose."

"No way! That's ridiculous," complained Trevor. "You're in your uniform. That's what you wear."

"Hey," said Jilly sternly, "do you want your photo or not?"

"I don't care," replied Trevor in a sullen voice. "He asked you, not me."

Suddenly I could see my end result fading. Now there was a new obstacle in my way. Not Jilly, the object of the plan, but Trevor, my ally in the plan. I began to form ideas about what I could say to him that would induce him to go along with her condition. I found myself favoring the idea of pointing out to him that this was all his idea, and that he would be defeating the very vision he had proposed if he chickened out.

I was about to say this to Trevor when it occurred to me that what I was trying to do was force him to support the vision by shaming him. It was strange to see Trevor in his swing circle, but that was where he was, and I realized it had thrown me back into mine. From everything I had just learned, I appreciated that I stood a better chance of getting this photo if I went back to the obvious action that needed to be taken, rather than do what I believed would manipulate Trevor into compliance.

What, I asked myself, was the obvious? I looked back at Trevor and imagined Jilly sitting on his lap, both of them naked. As I did so, it occurred to me that Jilly had already asked him to take his clothes off. There was nothing for me to do.

Jilly and Trevor stared at each other obstinately. I reflected on the tension I would normally have experienced as a result of two people's wills clashing, but in that moment I felt relaxed. According to the fourth secret of magic, there was nothing for me to do other than hold the vision. What I wanted was in Jilly's and Trevor's hands. All I could do was trust they each had a heart.

The tension was unexpectedly broken by my friend at the next table. It seemed he and his companions had been following the events at our table. "Come on," said the man, "be a sport. It's only fair what she's asking."

"Yeah," the others said, adding their encouragement. "Come on, be a man. What are you afraid of?"

"Don't be a pussy."

"I'll take my clothes off," volunteered the man who had previously invited Jilly to sit on his lap.

Slowly, very slowly, a grin began to show on Trevor's face. "All right," he snapped at the next table, "I'll do it." To which they all gave a big cheer. "But," he said to Jilly, "I'm keeping my boxers on. That's fair."

"Ugh! As long as they don't touch me," laughed Jilly. "Now come on, get it off, buster."

Unlike every other patron in the Bull Market, Trevor was not wearing a suit. He was dressed casually in a pair of jeans and a silk shirt. After he had unlaced and taken off his running shoes, it took him only a few seconds to take the rest of his clothes off. The guys at the next table all whooped and cheered their approval. More than one comment was made about Trevor's skinny, pigeon-chested physique and his milk-bottle white skin, no doubt a legacy of a life spent indoors in front of a computer screen.

Trevor bowed to the next table, then went up to the balustrade and began doing muscleman poses for the benefit of the crowd below. For a moment, the hall really did fall silent as everyone's attention was drawn to the pale, rangy man dressed in only a pair of shiny boxer shorts, flexing his scrawny muscles at them. Once everyone had taken the scene in, and realized who it was, a roar of appreciation went up, interspersed with wolf whistles and calls for Trevor to lose the boxers as well. And then Jilly went up to the balustrade and, putting her left arm around Trevor's neck and pushing her ample chest out, flexed her right bicep. The crowd went berserk.

I called to Trevor and Jilly to turn around, which they did after a while, and I took a few shots of them clowning arm in arm. Then Trevor swooped Jilly up in his arms, and I got a photo of the tall, skinny nerd staggering under the weight of the voluptuous tanned blonde.

Above the din of the crowd, one voice could be heard

calling out above the others. There was a hush as it became apparent whom the voice belonged to. It was Stavros, the thug-like proprietor. For a moment, I thought there was going to be trouble, but it soon became clear what his excitement was about. He was waving a digital camera at us from the floor below and didn't want anyone to move until he could get up to the mezzanine and get a few shots for himself.

By the time Stavros reached our table, Jilly and Trevor had been joined spontaneously by Karen and another wait-ress. A few other people came forward with cameras and asked if they could take photos, and Trevor obliged the pho-tographers with a series of satirical bodybuilding poses, with the women either hanging off him or striking their own over-the-top vogue postures.

Our shenanigans had transformed the Bull Market into a gigantic party. It was as if Trevor's actions had given every-one permission to cut loose. Hardly anyone sat down again. Patrons mingled on the floor of the great hall, introducing themselves to strangers and laughing about the scene they had just witnessed. Wanting to be at the center of the action, people drifted up to the mezzanine to chat with acquaintances or introduce themselves to total strangers. Eventually, they all made their way to pay tribute to Trevor, who by now had put his clothes back on. It didn't take long for word to spread that it was I who had instigated the lark, and everyone began treating me like the hero of the day. Waitresses stopped to put an arm around me and find out if there was anything I wanted. Patrons came over to slap me on the back and, in spite of my objections, order me a drink. Our table was crammed with full tankards of beer, shot glasses of spirits, and psychedelic cocktails of every description.

I caught Trevor's eye and motioned with my head to all the drinks laid out in front of us. He picked up a random glass of something and held it up in a toast. "Well," he declared, "we're not resolving tension now, are we? We're celebrating. Here's to magic."

I felt an enormous sense of relief as I picked up a strange-looking liqueur — not for the sake of the drink, but to acknowledge the completion of the incredible transformation we had both effected over lunch. "Cheers," I replied, grinning with immense pleasure.

Stavros stood nearby looking satisfied as he watched his waitresses trying to cope with the frenzied demand for drinks. After a while, he pulled up a chair next to me and sat down. "Ah, it's okay," he sighed. "It's all okay." He considered me for a moment and said, "You're a Svengali, eh, Mr. Information Man?"

"What's that?" I said.

"You have power over people." His tone implied I knew very well what he meant.

I looked back at him and, raising my glass, said with cheerful flattery, "But you're the king, Stavros. You're the king."

That brought an even happier glow to the publican's face. Trevor winked at me and asked, "So, Svengali, what would you love now?"

"To take the rest of the day off," I replied, loosening my tie.

IN ANOTHER WORLD

Trevor had said that I wouldn't recognize my own life by nightfall, but I doubt he himself could have predicted the incredible series of events that would unfold after he uttered those prophetic words. Not more than five minutes after I'd declared my desire to take the rest of the afternoon off, my next appointment called me on my mobile phone to cancel our meeting. Rather than being disappointed, I was relieved. The acquisitions librarian at the Continental Group of companies, whom I was supposed to be meeting after lunch, behaved more like a pit bull guarding the company's coffers than the administrator of the group's information resources.

The Continental Group, which controlled a conglomeration of financial services organizations that included banks, brokerage houses, insurance companies, and fund managers, was something of an anomaly in the financial markets in that it was still run the way companies had been run twenty or thirty years earlier, before global deregulation. In every other organization, even government departments, the executives I dealt with enjoyed a fair degree of autonomy and had the discretion to subscribe to whatever information they wanted out of their own budgets. Even though the Continental Group was the ultimate capitalistic institution, everything in it was centrally planned and controlled like a Marxist state. All information was acquired through the group library. Not even the most senior economists, research directors, or planning strategists had the authority to decide for themselves what they could subscribe to.

Bearing this in mind, you would have thought that the Continental library would be a convenient and lucrative source of business for me. However, the opposite was true. I hadn't sold a single subscription or report to anyone in the empire for four years. The chief librarian, it seemed, had decided that the executives within her organization needed to be protected from the decadent excesses of external analysis and opinion — a bourgeois extravagance, like designer clothing or à la carte restaurants. What her clients didn't know they were missing couldn't hurt them. No need to open the floodgates of extravagant expenditure or add to her department's workload!

The last thing the Continental librarian wanted was a guy like me hanging around with an enticing catalogue of services touching on the heart of her clients' crucial interests. I was under strict orders to approach no one in the group other than the acquisitions librarian, or I would be blacklisted by the entire organization forever. Why they even bothered with the courtesy of tolerating my half-yearly approaches I wasn't quite sure. I could only suspect it was to deceive me into the delusion that there might be some hope for me as long as I toed their line and didn't bother the business units directly. That, and to get copies of my new catalogue from me to burn.

One of the things I enjoyed about my job was that even if my clients or prospects were adequately covered or didn't have room in their budgets, everyone I dealt with appreciated the service I provided and acknowledged the value of the information I supplied. Everyone, that is, except the Continental acquisitions librarian. The contempt with which she treated me would have led you to believe I was promoting one of those Nigerian money-laundering scams. It was clear from her attitude that she was just looking for an excuse never to have to deal with me again.

So I was understandably relieved when she phoned to say she'd been called away to a family crisis and begrudgingly requested that I call her the following day to reschedule our appointment. The only reason I bothered to suffer her condescension was that I was patiently biding my time until the library lost its power. It was only a matter of time before the Continental Group joined the twenty-first century and decentralized control. And with the information vacuum that existed in the entire organization, I stood to make a small fortune if I played my cards right. There was probably a year's worth of new sales to be made in one fell swoop. What I stood to earn would simply be a function of how quickly I could write out the orders.

But that time, as far as I was aware, wasn't now. So I was happy to express my insincere regrets that we wouldn't be meeting that afternoon, and raised a fresh glass of un-identified alcoholic substance to the latest toast being pro-posed within the vicinity of our table. The responding cheers had hardly died down when the imposing figure of a man dressed in an immaculate Italian suit and exquisite silk tie loomed over us.

"Gentlemen," he said, "may I join you?" It wasn't so much a request as a statement of intention. He didn't intro-duce himself, because he didn't need any introduction. He was Digby Wallace, the executive chairman of the Conti-nental Group of companies.

"Um, pah-pahlease sit down," I stammered as he eased his substantial frame into a seat at our table. The chair creaked apprehensively beneath him as he shifted around to establish optimum comfort. Digby Wallace was in no way obese, but he had that fleshy, florid look a man of his stature develops on the corporate entertainment circuit. There was an aura about him common to famous or highly successful people that somehow makes you appreciate their every gesture and com-ment and compels you to want to do anything to please them.

"Stavros," nodded the tycoon, acknowledging the pro-prietor, who, although he was sitting with us, was in fact in a world of his own, with his mind squarely focused on busi-ness. The banker turned his attention to Trevor. "Mr. Campbell," he said, as if he were informing Trevor of his own name, "I've heard a lot about you. I must say, I admire your reputation."

"Good of you to join us, Digby," replied Trevor affably. "Help yourself to a drink." He waved his hand at the fifteen or so untouched drinks on our table before taking the chairman of Continental's outstretched hand.

"I think I'll finish this one first." Digby Wallace held up a tumbler of whiskey that looked like a thimble in his hand. "Then I'll be happy to help you boys clear your table." He used a dry tone of voice that managed to communicate two things simultaneously. One, he was a no-crap kind of guy, and two, he thought we were okay. It was part of that aura that made you feel privileged to be in his company.

Once I'd stated my name and offered my hand to be crushed in his vice-like grip, Digby Wallace turned his attention fully to Trevor and began quizzing the world champion on his opinion of the current state of the international money markets. As I sat there listening to them talk, I couldn't help but marvel that I was sitting at the same table as the chief executive of the organization whose business I had been fantasizing about for four years now. I reflected with a great deal of satisfaction that, had the Continental librarian not called to cancel, I would be heading over to her office right now to be treated like dirt, when here I was being helped by her boss to knock back the oversupply of drinks I'd been bought as a mark of respect from the very class of people she was an underling to. What an amazing coincidence, I thought, that my meeting with the librarian was off, yet here I was hob-nobbing with the chairman of her company. I couldn't see how that would help me get any business, but it did make me feel good. Especially after four drinks.

As pleased as I was at the company I was keeping, it wasn't long before I began to feel like a third wheel, as Digby Wallace and Trevor became immersed in their private tête-à-tête. I did try to contribute to their conversation. After all, it was my job to keep up-to-date with the markets and what the major pundits were saying about them. But a scholar's opinion never carries much weight with those whose livelihood depends on the subject being discussed. So, while my comments did distract the other two momentarily, it wasn't long before they were off and running on another tangent that left me studiously examining the ice in my drink.

I had just reached the point where I was beginning to feel uncomfortably self-conscious when the big man switched his attention to me. After nodding his head vigorously in agreement with some point Trevor had made, Digby Wallace looked the table over and selected a drink that most closely resembled whiskey. He held it up to his nose and sniffed it suspiciously before breaking out in a broad smile.

"Ah, someone's got good taste." He nodded his head in approval. "Thanks, boys." He held his glass up to us, and then, to me, he said, "I've got a challenge for you, son."

"For me?" I stuttered. "What sort of challenge?"

"Well," the tycoon grimaced, "it's a pretty big one, but I think you can handle it. Want to hear it?"

"Okay," I responded, wondering what the hell I was getting myself into while at the same time eager to please the legendary billionaire, especially now that he was giving me the time of day.

"It's like this," he said gravely. "Tonight I'm hosting a party on my yacht for Melissa Matheson. This evening we're unveiling the mural she painted in the foyer of our head office. Now, I don't know if you know Melissa," the big man looked at me as though I was bound to, "but she's a lively girl, and the guest list is a who's who of stuffed shirts — you know, old farts, every one of them. So I've been trying to get these two young birds to come along and brighten things up for us."

Digby Wallace inclined his head in the direction of Jilly and Karen, who were standing nearby sorting out the discrepancy in a patron's bill. Feeling our eyes on them, both waitresses looked up at the same time. Karen poked her tongue out at us playfully, and the two of them looked back down at the bill again. Their concentration was broken, however, and they began giggling over some facetious comment Jilly had made. The Continental chairman fixed the two of them with a forced smile and raised his glass to them. Turning back to Trevor and me, he muttered, "Yes, exactly. Nothing can persuade them. Everyone at my table has tried. They've been offered everything. They just won't come."

"So what do you want me to do about it?" I asked, genuinely intrigued as to how I could help him.

"Well, isn't it obvious?" said the big man smoothly. "Your challenge, should you accept it, is to get them to come along to the party. They are bound to be amenable to your approach — you being the man of the hour."

I thought about his request for a moment. I was truly flattered that this larger-than-life figure assumed I had the power to do what he and his boardroom cronies had failed to do. At the same time, the thought of pimping for these corporate fat cats turned my stomach. The last thing I wanted to do was begin hustling two people whose trust, respect, and, dare I think it, affection, I had just gained.

"The only way I'd be able to do it is if I were invited to the party," I said.

"Of course, of course," said the Continental chairman. "That goes without saying. You're both invited — with or without the girls. You boys look like you know how to liven up a party."

"Okay then," I said, warming to the challenge, "let's see what I can do."

As I stood up to walk over to Karen and Jilly, I saw a look of innocent pleasure beaming from Digby Wallace's face. It occurred to me that this must be a rare moment of real fun in what must otherwise be a routinely serious existence for the great man. "The third secret of magic," I thought to myself. "Everyone has a heart."

I was surprised at how unsteady I was on my feet. The quick succession of drinks I had downed had done nothing for my balance. Jilly and Karen grabbed each other in alarm as I lurched toward them. "Are you all right?" asked Jilly, her face showing mild concern as I rocked unsteadily in front of her.

"Never felt better," I assured her with a reckless smile. "Just stood up too fast."

"What can we do for you?" said Karen.

"Well, as a matter of fact, I was wondering if you knew about Digby's party tonight?" I asked.

Jilly let out a groan of disgust. "Did that creep get you to come and ask us again?"

"Well, he did," I admitted. "But that's not why I'm here."

"It's not?" Jilly's eyes opened wide in exaggerated anticipation.

"No," I explained. "I haven't come to persuade you to go to Digby's party. I wanted to see if you'd like to do something fun tonight. As it happens, there's a party for Melissa Matheson on Digby's yacht. I think it'll be an amazing night. I'd love it if you guys came along. Then I'd have some great company. I'd be with friends."

"You're serious, aren't you?" said Jilly, her whole demeanor softening.

"Melissa Matheson! The artist?" Karen's tone betrayed her sudden interest.

"That's right, the artist," I said, raising my level of enthusiasm again.

"They didn't say anything about it being a party for Melissa Matheson," frowned Jilly. "All those guys were going on about was how big and lavish the boat was, and how much champagne and caviar there'd be, and how they'd pick us up in a limo. They even promised us a big tip if we went along. Stupid creeps!"

"Look," I said soothingly, "it's not at all sinister. That's just how they think they've got to appeal to you. They think it's about impressing people. Instead, they've put you off a perfectly straight-up event. They're going to be there with their wives, and the mayor is going to be there, and the director of the national gallery. I mean, imagine who goes to these things: business tycoons, movie stars, people from the arts. They're inviting you because they think you're cool. It's a compliment. They've just got a crude way of expressing it." Listening to myself speak, I wondered where my words were coming from.

"So you're going?" Jilly's resistance had all but melted.

"For sure!" I cried. "I've never been to a high-society event like this before. You should come along. It's just an opportunity to have a great time."

"All right, I'm in." Karen held up her hand for me to high five.

"Melissa Matheson," cooed Jilly, "she's cool." She grabbed my arm in excitement. "Hey, I'm sure Helena would love to come." Helena was the other waitress who had posed with Trevor.

I was completely elated at the prospect of going to Digby Wallace's party accompanied by the three most heavenly creatures I'd ever met. A thrill ran up and down my spine and finally emerged from my mouth as a high-pitched squeak, as if someone had run a violin bow across my vocal chords. As tipsy as I was, I was still sober enough to be embarrassed by this involuntary vocal spasm. Suddenly I didn't feel so cool. I mumbled something about how delighted I was that they would be coming along after all and dashed back to my table.

Afraid that my excitement would burst out of me and

cause me to do something silly, I sat down as quickly as I could and grabbed the nearest drink. I emptied it down my throat in one go, hoping it would calm me down — which it almost did. I had to have another shot of something before I felt satisfactorily sedated.

Digby Wallace eyed me with concern. "Not go well, huh?" he queried. "From what I saw, it seemed like you were doing okay."

I emptied the second glass and looked him steadily in the eye. "We need five invitations to your party," I said as coolly as I could. "And we'll need that limo you promised them."

The look of childish pleasure rose like the sun on Digby's face again. "Excellent," he laughed, clapping his hands together in appreciation. "Well done."

"And they'll take you up on that big tip," I said as an afterthought.

Digby motioned for one of his party to come over and whispered instructions in the man's ear. The man nodded as his boss spoke. With a starchy "Very good, sir," the man went over to the women and, pulling a pen and notebook from the breast pocket of his jacket, began writing down whatever details they were offering him. I looked at my watch. It was time for me to head off to my second afternoon appointment.

I tried to stand up but didn't get far. As I collapsed back into my chair, the whole world began to spin beneath me. It was as though all the excitement of the last twenty-four hours, and all the stress of being in the Bull Market, and the seven or eight drinks I'd sunk in the last forty-five minutes, had all come crashing down on my head in a single blow. I felt nauseously dizzy, and a throbbing ache had made its way into my skull and settled behind my right eye.

"Are you okay?" I heard Trevor's voice echoing through the fog that had set in around me. I wanted to say, "Not really," but I didn't trust myself to open my mouth. I was absolutely certain that if I did, it would be the end of me. I imagined myself disappearing in an explosion of vomit and humiliation. Even breathing was making me feel sicker.

"Just hang in there." I heard Trevor get up and a chain reaction of curious solicitude break out around me.

"What's up?"

"Is he okay?"

"Drink those cocktails too fast?"

"Who's going to get him out of here?"

Every voice was like a missile exploding against my head. I felt terrible. Besides the pain and nausea was the guilt at the certainty I would miss my appointments that afternoon, and the disappointment of losing out on my coveted invitation to Digby Wallace's party. Helping me feel even worse was the thought of how pathetic I must have looked to the two big men at our table, Stavros and the Continental chairman.

After what seemed like an excruciating amount of time, a soothing voice came floating sweetly through the fog. This voice didn't hurt my head; the very sound of it stroked and calmed my mind. It had that nurturing quality sick children recognize in their mother or nurse. Whoever it belonged to pulled up a chair and sat down beside me.

"Okay, what have we got here?" It was Jilly, her voice a mixture of business-like pragmatism and gentle compassion. As comforting as her presence was, I still didn't dare speak. All I managed was an involuntary groan. "Oh, dear," Jilly sympathized. She softly held my face in her hands. The warmth of her femininity washed through me. Sick as I was, something Trevor had said came back to me. Something about there being things only a woman could teach me. Only a woman could have such a healing effect, I thought. "Migraine, nausea, dehydration, severe toxicity." Even Jilly's mechanical assessment of my condition had an enchanting ring to it. Her presence made me feel much better.

"Let's see what we can do here," said Jilly. She removed her hands from my face by sliding her fingers slowly down my cheeks. Then she began massaging my brow ever so gently. She only did that for about a minute before she pressed her thumbs across my eyebrows three times. Finally, she tapped on my forehead with her fingernails. "There, that ought to do it," she announced.

With the last tap I felt every scintilla of pain and discomfort drain from my head in an instant. For a second there, I thought I was totally fine, until I felt the most incredible nausea sitting in my throat. To my horror, I realized I was about to do the biggest vomit in history, and that nothing was going to save me.

"Obviously not!" Jilly cried in panic. She quickly jabbed my chest three times with her fingertips just above my solar plexus. The pain of her jabs popped my eyes open wide to see her studying my face intently. "Ah, that's done it," she pronounced.

The bilious feeling in my throat sank down my esophagus to I don't know where. It simply vanished. I was fine. I felt pretty much the way I had before I'd touched the first drink; maybe even better — my mind felt fresh and clear.

"He's okay. Must have stood up too fast," Digby Wallace rationalized on behalf of the crowd. To me he chortled, "Christ, son, you had me worried there for a minute. Thought you couldn't hold your liquor."

This comment drew a surprising amount of laughter. Either it was that eagerness to please powerful individuals, or the boys in the Bull Market were strongly identified with drinking. It was probably both. "You know how a French woman holds her liquor?" piped up the man who had earlier incurred Jilly's wrath. "By the ears!" It was an old joke, but the crowd loved it all the same.

"That's right," I thought, "they're drunk and I'm not."

Jilly was still sitting beside me. I could sense she was intentionally there to support me through the shock of being so suddenly jolted back into sobriety. "Thanks, Jilly." I didn't know how to express my gratitude; I was completely flabbergasted. "How the . . . how did you do that?"

"People aren't always what they seem," she answered mysteriously.

"What?" My mind began reeling again.

Jilly arched her eyebrows as if to imply there was more to her than I could ever imagine. Before I could engage her, she was up. "I'll see you tonight," she smiled. Then, like a magician's assistant, she was gone, disappearing into the clouds of cigar smoke.

I looked vacantly about me. Stavros had disappeared, too. Digby Wallace stood surrounded by a throng of eager sycophants, rewarding each deserving attendant with a throaty chuckle and a slap on the back. Their faces lit up as he graced them with his special favor, and then dimmed again once his attention moved on to the next ingratiating subject. Trevor appeared at the edge of the crowd, beckoning me with a nod of his head. Time to go.

Leaving the Bull Market and stepping back out onto the street was a bit like crossing over from one world to another. I fantasized that if I went back and knocked on the door, I'd be met by an old man who'd swear there was nothing down below except the defunct boiler room of the high-rise above. And that if I went back with the correct password, I could pay my money and walk down the stairs and have my whole life's psychological journey play out in an hour or two, depending which package I chose.

BY THE TIME I'D BEEN TO MY FIVE APPOINTMENTS for the afternoon, driven back to Cliff's house — picking up a dinner suit from a formal-wear rental shop on the way — and showered and changed, the Bull Market had faded into a questionable memory in my mind. The ordinariness of my old routine quickly claimed me back, and the extraordinary world I had visited for lunch was already like a freakish blip on a radar screen. I had already lost touch with what had been so incredible about my experience. Until I answered the doorbell at seven that evening.

The sight that greeted me made me recoil back into the hallway a few paces trying to get my arrested breath going again. Standing there in the doorway was Jilly, dressed in a skimpy sheath of ice-like material and a pair of stilettos that looked as if they'd been carved out of a block of mirrored glass. She looked even more stunning with clothes on than she had half naked. What she wore suggested that a bounty from heaven lay underneath, and her luscious makeup highlighted her features in an inhumanly beautiful face. I was totally awestruck, as if I were in the presence of Aphrodite reincarnated in the twenty-first century.

"Hey, Svengali, let's rock and roll!" she laughed, gaily offering me her arm.

Climbing into the plush padded cell of the stretch limousine, I was transported right back to the Bull Market. There were the women — Jilly, Karen, and Helena — all made over in the designer version of the unattainable trophy goddess. There was the television monitor again, charging the atmosphere with the swaggering groove of some rapper invoking the power of lust and greed and violence. And there was Trevor dressed in a tuxedo with a paisley cummerbund, sitting with the amused detachment of an ambassador in the court of a lesser kingdom, holding out an offering of champagne for me. The comfortable leather cocoon shielded us from the messy struggle of the world beyond. The smooth motion of the limo and the giddy laughter of the women added to the feeling that we were being inexorably drawn into some dimension so special that only those handpicked by Aaron Spelling could exist there.

The same fear and loathing that had at first come over me in the Bull Market now took control of my senses again. The vision of Digby surrounded by his fawning admirers came back to me, and I suddenly became annoyed that I would soon be among so many desperate souls clambering to be within reach of the man with the Midas touch. I felt disdain for the women, disappointment that they would so eagerly play the role of disposable toys for the champions of such a shallow quest. I had already forgotten that we were all there as a result of my need for the Continental chief's approval.

This time, however, I didn't take myself too seriously. I simply allowed myself to listen to my thoughts and feelings. Doing so, I quickly realized once again that I was assuming that it was all a giant competition and that I wasn't worthy or powerful enough to compete. My own assumptions of inadequacy were resolving themselves by making me want to separate myself from the situation I found myself in.

Seeing my assumptions for what they so clearly were allowed me to take back my judgments of everyone and recognize that there was actually nothing wrong with them. People were simply living their lives, and any problem I had with them was born of the notion that their behavior threatened my existence in some way. Digby, Trevor, the women, their admirers and suitors — they were all just doing their thing, not maliciously trying to destroy me!

As soon as I could see that none of the partygoers were in truth a threat to me, I warmed to my companions all over again. I could see their hearts again. I could feel all of their beauty and sensuality and intelligence and capability and creativity and love and playfulness searching feverishly for avenues of expression, and I felt a pang of guilt that I would begrudge them that expression so that I could feel better. In that moment, I knew once again that what I ultimately wanted was simply to connect with and share that passion, not dominate it. I surrendered to the mood in the back of the limo and swayed from side to side with Helena and Jilly, as everyone yelled out the chorus of the video clip and held out their glasses for Trevor to refill.

When we finally arrived at the pier where Digby's yacht was moored, we ran into a large throng of guests too busy greeting each other like long-lost friends to have made it up the gangway. Evenly distributed throughout the crowd was a fair smattering of faces I recognized from television and the Sunday papers: a breakfast radio king; a few actors and soap stars; a late-night newsreader; a columnist or two; some well-known CEOs and their spouses, famous in their own right as corporate players or for their high-profile charity work; the mayor, joking with a network finance editor while a society hairdresser gushed over their wives; and, surrounded by a coterie of highly contrived bohemians, the guest of honor herself, Melissa Matheson. In among them all, a large contingent of paparazzi feasted on the smorgasbord of photo opportunities.

It took us only about five seconds to lose the women.

They were sucked into the vortex of glamour like light disappearing into a black hole in space. Trevor and I skirted around the glittering mob and headed for the gangway. After having our invitations checked by a cordon of uniformed police officers and dark-suited security agents, we went on board.

I thought the security arrangements were excessive for a private function, but I soon realized this was no ordinary party. When someone says "yacht," I tend to think of something like an oceangoing sailboat or a large cabin cruiser. Neither image did any justice to Digby Wallace's yacht. I'd seen photos of it in magazines, and I knew it was big, but in real life it resembled a modern-day warship stripped of its battle stations and weapons systems. As we climbed up the stairs, I could make out the silhouette of a helicopter on an upper rear deck, and on the deck below that, shadows danced at the bottom of a brightly lit swimming pool. Cantilevered over the back of the yacht was a fair-sized motor launch, no doubt used as a runabout in whatever exotic bays the vessel moored in.

My surprise at the external dimensions of the ship was nothing compared to my astonishment at seeing the interior, which was designed to give one the impression of being inside the type of luxury hotel favored by the royal families of oil-rich nations. Once on board, we entered a palm-filled lobby where a trio of smiling uniformed crew members stationed behind an elaborately carved reception desk pointed us in the direction of a wide, richly carpeted staircase. Crossing a marble expanse furnished with clusters of black leather lounges and easy chairs, we followed the stairs up to another plush foyer-like area attended by more uniformed crew standing like sentinels on either side of a set of imposing, gold-leafed ebony doors. As we approached, they silently pulled the doors open for us, revealing the chandeliered ballroom beyond.

Inside the ornate ballroom, a dozen waiters and chefs busied themselves around ice and food sculptures. Not many guests had arrived yet. In fact, the numbers were confined to a small group of stylishly dressed matrons conversing in the center of the room, a few of whom looked familiar, and an equivalent number of middle-aged men guffawing loudly at the bar. I immediately recognized three of the men: a high-profile corporate counsel, Digby Wallace, and the prime minister, whose presence explained the large security contingent on the quay.

Trevor walked over to the bar without breaking his stride. I found myself lagging behind. If ever I had felt out of my depth, it was now. Me, a humble newsletter-subscription salesman, surrounded by men who had the power to go to war with other countries — and did; men who employed tens of thousands of people; and men who shuffled the nation's wealth around and split it between themselves. I imagined myself as some impostor who had penetrated the inner sanctum of the ruling elite. This was the furthest I'd ever strayed from my own universe, and now I wondered, with no small amount of trepidation, how far I could run before I would be cornered and squashed like a bug.

If the water-palace setting was a pharaoh-like display

of power designed to shock and awe the plebes, it certainly worked on me. Not Trevor, though. He walked straight up to the country's A-team and introduced himself. "So when do the strippers come on, Digby?" he asked loudly, drawing a few chuckles from the small group of men.

"I don't know," replied our host agreeably. "I thought you guys were bringing them." He then introduced me to the group: "This is Mark Vale." With a laugh, he said, "Mark is the man to talk to about women. We call him 'Svengali' down at the Bull Market."

"The Bull Market?" bawled the prime minister. "I think I've heard of that. Is that the place where you get your pound of flesh with your steak, so to speak?"

Everyone laughed knowingly. "Good fox-hunting venue," said the corporate lawyer dryly.

I leaned up against the bar and asked for a glass of champagne. The feeling of intimidation I had at being in the presence of such exalted company melted away. In one deft stroke Trevor had cut through the imposing, armor-plated veneer of superiority to reveal the common blood that flowed through the veins of these hallowed beings. I reminded myself that I was here to enjoy the spectacle of a five-star event, not to measure up to anything. A shiver of excitement ran through my body. I felt drawn to go stand outside and take in the city's lights shining on the water before the star-studded crowd came spilling onboard and wrecked the stillness of the night.

I was on the deck behind the ballroom foyer, staring across the bay to the prime minister's harborside lodge, when the voices of Digby Wallace and Trevor Campbell reached me.

"It's a sad world when a man can't smoke inside his own boat, I tell you!" grumbled the Continental chief.

"I know, Digby. I was going to ask you: who wears the pants in your house?" said Trevor, nudging the big man playfully in the ribs.

"I do, of course... when my wife lets me." The big man's hearty burst of laughter tailed off into a smoker's cough. "Ah, Svengali, there you are," he said, recovering his breath. "What happened to the girls?"

"They're here," I replied. "But it doesn't look like you really needed my help to pull in the beautiful people."

"Ah, well," said Digby. "As tonight's event attests, I'm an art lover." He took a deep drag on his cigarette. "What's your line of business, Svengali?"

"I sell business information. Economic and financial analysis." I was aware of not sounding confident that this would be a substantial enough occupation in the big man's eyes.

He must have picked up on my insecurity. "Well, you know, I started out as a bank teller," he said. "You probably deal with a lot of my people."

"Not really," I said.

"How's that?" the Continental chief demanded.

"Because you guys live in the dark ages, Digby!" Trevor exclaimed in that deriding tone people usually use only with their closest friends.

"What do you mean?" said the big man easily.

"I deal with analysts and traders in every Continental arm, and I'll tell you straight, Digby, your boys are famous for being out of touch with the markets and behind the times in their methods." All the time, Trevor kept his tone light. "They don't have access to external information like everyone else. They're working in the dark."

"How come?" asked Digby.

Trevor deferred to me for the answer. I was cringing at what he'd been telling the big man. The last thing I wanted to do was insult the pharaoh on his state barge, but I had resolved to be myself tonight, and damn the consequences. I took a deep breath and blurted out my reply. "Well, all information acquisitions are controlled by the group library. Technically the librarians are supposed to look after the users' needs, but in effect they only frustrate them. Your librarians are like cooks in the army judging what ordnance the frontline troops can fight their wars with. Analysts or strategists might want the benefit of some service, but they just get told there isn't enough support in the group, or there isn't room in the budget. How would the information users know whether that's true or not? Mostly they don't even know what information is available."

"And you know what the joke is, Digby?" Trevor said, cutting in. "The joke is that this retarded measure is designed to save the equivalent of an economist's salary, in an organization that employs upward of twenty thousand people."

Digby Wallace took a last puff on his cigarette and flicked it carelessly out into the harbor. "Well, that's easily fixed," he said, straightening himself up and turning his gaze from Trevor to me. "From tomorrow you deal with whomever you like in Continental, boy. As long as something comes out of a department's own budget, there can't be any harm in it. Now, if you'll excuse me, I have to mingle."

I held my breath until I was sure Digby was well inside, and then I let out a scream of delight. The last time I'd come close to feeling like this was when I'd survived going down a double-black-diamond run by mistake when I was still learning to ski. It was as if I'd won the lottery. Digby Wallace had just handed me a year's salary in two sentences. In an instant, the dark cloud of my unfathomable financial woes had been lifted and a bright, limitless future had opened up. Pure joy coursed through my veins, enlivening every single cell and fiber of my being.

Ignoring Trevor, I did a little jig around the deck and then let out another scream. "Can you believe that?" I yelled, coming back to Trevor. "Give me five, man!"

"I can believe it," laughed Trevor, slapping my hand high in the air.

"Well, I can't," I said hysterically. "I can't believe that I'm here on this boat. I can't believe that I pulled up here in a limo with three women most men would tear each other's throats out to be with. I can't believe I'm on this yacht at the same party as the prime minister. I can't believe I've just been handed a year's worth of business on a silver plate." I took a gulp of fresh air. "I can't believe it," I shouted. "How did I get here? This is too far up the food chain for a guy like me. This is too much at once. In my life you get a crumb at a time, not the whole cake."

Trevor laughed again. "Well, you're working with magic now," he said casually.

"What magic?" I cried. "What magic? I didn't focus on any of this. I didn't visualize any of this happening."

"Sure you did," said Trevor. "You've been dreaming of this your whole life. It's always been there. Today you just let yourself have it."

"What the hell are you talking about?" I snorted in bewilderment.

"Well, it's like this," explained Trevor. "Imagine you don't exist in one life only, that you exist in many lives simultaneously. For instance, there's the Mark who wakes up every morning and goes out knocking on doors to see who's got some scraps for him. He takes his lunch in the park with the pigeons, and then at night he goes to the movies with a friend. Things in his life are boring, but they're safe and predictable. He never puts himself in scary situations. His life is emotionally stable. The metaphor that springs to mind is that of a fisherman who never chases the fish out at sea. He just goes fishing off the beach in fine weather, casting his line into the surf and hoping something will bite.

"Then there's the Mark who doesn't play it as safe as he can. He doesn't just throw his line in the water and hope. He watches the sea and looks for where the birds are diving. He follows the action. He goes out to sea in rough weather. He's at the mercy of the elements. He stands to get torn apart at any moment. But he's not in it for the scraps. When he sails back into harbor, his boat is groaning with the richest catch imaginable.

"You see, Mark is living these lives, and more, every day. The life he chooses to stand in, on any given day, is the life he experiences. Today you stepped out of Mark the Worrywart's world into Mark the Warrior's world. And look, the night is still young and you've already hauled in that catch."

"But wasn't it all just luck?" I argued. "Wasn't it just luck that I met Digby, and that I got invited here, and that you were here to tell him how stupid Continental's subscription policy is? I mean, I didn't intend any of it; I didn't visualize or focus on any of these things happening."

"Nor did you have to," replied Trevor. "Living your life by magic doesn't mean keeping an unbroken line of sight between yourself and specific things you want. Living by magic is about setting up structures."

"Structures?"

"Structures. The fifth secret of magic: Structure has integrity. That means that the nature of a structure determines consistent and predictable outcomes."

"For example?"

"For example, a square block will tend to remain inert. A ball will tend to roll. Do what you like to get a square block rolling; it will always come to rest. Try to stop a ball rolling, and it won't stand still for long. Something's structure determines its behavior, and its behavior determines its experience."

Trevor didn't get a response from me — I was too busy digesting what he was saying — so he went on.

"What I'm talking about here goes to the very heart of

change. You see, when you go for things in life, nothing's going to change unless the underlying structure changes. It's like with golf. Think about all the years you tried to improve your golf game, and look what happened. Nothing. Why? Because you were stuck in the old paradigm of technique. But then you changed the structure. You shifted your focus from the process to the end result. And look what happened. Breakthrough!

"If the structure is wrong, it doesn't matter what you do right — the result will be ordinary. And if the structure is right, it doesn't matter what you do wrong — the result will be great. If there's no shift, it's because the structure hasn't changed, that's all. And that goes for every single thing in life: health, wealth, relationships, sales, politics, spirituality, artistic endeavor — you name it.

"So never say that today was just luck. Every day your natural ability is lining up the most remarkable sequence of events. Today you just happened to capitalize on that reality."

I still couldn't see what I'd done to effect the windfall that had just landed in my lap. "But you said that your focus creates your reality," I objected, "and I didn't focus on coming to this party or getting Continental's business."

"Nonsense," scoffed Trevor. "You've been focused on making money. That's what you're doing in town. And you've been focused on Continental for four years. You've been drooling over it like a dog outside a butcher's shop. Your natural ability is constantly creating avenues to get that business and make more money. You're just getting in the way all the time."

"How do I do that?" I asked.

"Well, let's take it back to what you told me about golf. What you discovered was that you had the natural ability to hit a perfectly good shot, right? Also, you realized you'd been getting in the way of your natural ability by imposing technique on it. So the same goes for everything else in life. Your natural ability is sitting there, waiting to produce the results you're looking for, but you're often in the way. Except today you got out of the way.

"Now, how did you get out of the way? I'll tell you. There was something you were focused on that freed you from your old paradigm. You were focused on staying in your heart. Every time you came back to your heart, you realized that all you wanted to do was connect with others and share their passion for life. You let go of your ancient assumption that life is a competition. And because you weren't competing, your fear didn't come up. And because your fear didn't come up, you didn't run away. You kept going. You stayed in the flow of what your natural ability was setting up. You see, you changed the structure, and that changed the behavior, which ultimately changed your experience."

I could vaguely see that I'd done something different that day, although I couldn't understand what structure I was supposed to have created. "So I stayed focused on my heart?" I puzzled. "What was the structure I set up?"

"That's it," said Trevor. "Being focused on your heart. The values you live by form the underlying structure in your consciousness. Your values are what you're making life about. They define your orientation in life, and your orientation determines consistent and predictable outcomes in life."

Trevor laughed softly to himself. Looking over at him, I could see he was recalling some profound memory. "I remember when I started trading," he reminisced. "I used to read everything I could on the subject. I studied every technical formula and digested every bit of supply-and-demand data. I memorized the effect that every major event had had on every market in the last hundred years. I tried to figure out every way I could cover my bets. I studied the cash preservation strategies of every great trader of the last century. I busted my ass trying to figure out how to succeed in those markets.

"Then one day I was sitting on a park bench running a slide rule over my charts when this bum came and sat down beside me. I don't remember him looking at what I was doing, but after a while he said to me, 'Hey, buddy, want to know the secret of trading?' The guy was a bum, right. I mean, he was dressed in rags and his face was blue. You wouldn't have relied on him to tell you if it was night or day, but I didn't want to hurt his feelings, so I asked him what it was. 'There's only one secret to trading,' he told me. 'Everything you do won't count for nothing if your intention is wrong. If you don't get that right, it'll chew you up and spit you out in little pieces you'll never be able to put together again. It's all about intention.'

"That's what he said. And I didn't have the slightest idea what he was talking about. But, you know, a few days later it hit me like a diamond bullet in the brain. Intention! Why are you trading? Where are you coming from? Are you trying to prove yourself to your father? Are you trying to make up for a loss? Are you trying to get rich quick? Are you greedy? Are you under pressure to make money for your clients? Are you afraid? Are you trying to avoid losing money? Or . . . are you trading because you love those markets? Because you have an affinity with them? Because you can see a blatantly obvious opportunity? In other words, is your motive pure?

"There's only one intention that's going to let you stay in touch with your natural ability and be one with the markets, and that's doing it for the pure reason that a great trade has presented itself. Any of the other intentions are going to automatically cause you to force the situation, and you'll inevitably end up in your swing circle. And, you see, all those different intentions are values. They're what you're making life about, what you're acting in favor of. And your values determine the outcome: there are true values, which engage your natural ability, and false values, which relegate you to your swing circle. The benefit of being aligned with your natural ability is that you tend to enjoy greater clarity and wisdom and take the most appropriate steps toward the end results you seek. Whereas when you are in your swing circle, your perception will be distorted and your actions will be dictated by what makes you feel good rather than what is truly in your highest interest.

"That's why magicians focus so heavily on structure. They don't care about their circumstances. They don't care if they win or lose, or if they laugh or cry. They're watching their motivations. Their job is to keep their intentions pure. Because they know that their values are ultimately responsible for whether they end up with what really matters to them in life."

I thought of Steve Addington and my first impression that he wasn't concerned about whether you hit a good shot or a bad one, or whether you were on time or not, that life was about something else for him. Now I knew what that was.

"So you see, Mark," Trevor said with a great depth of feeling, "if you want to live by magic, you have to change. There's no other way. You have to shift from false, fear-based values to true, love-based values. You can't stand in your old paradigm and hope to put a straw into the magician's world and suck life out of it.

"If you don't make that shift, and you go back to playing golf without Steve being there to hold you in the creative paradigm, your old structures based on fear of failure are going to pull you back into the swing circle no matter how hard you try to focus on the target. Then you'll start thinking that the magic isn't real, and you'll go out and look for a pro who can teach you a fail-safe technique. But what the real problem will be is that the underlying structure won't be aligned with the new level Steve has taken you to.

"If you want to sustain the magic you've been living by these last few days, you're going to have to learn how to identify the structures that are holding you back and find the structures that will take you forward. And then you'll have to find the will to let go of the old and embrace the new. And believe me, you'll need to master this ability if you want to stand half a chance with the next challenge that's waiting for you. It's going to make earning a year's salary in one day look like a walk in the park. I can sense some dark forces beginning to gather around you."

If I'd been in my normal state of mind, I probably would have been sobered by this ominous pronouncement. As it was, I was drunk on the delusion of power. I felt invincible, bulletproof, unstoppable. There was no force in the world that could deny me what I wanted.

"Thanks for the encouragement, comrade," I said flippantly.

Trevor was about to respond, but I saw him think better of it and let it go. "What the hell," he said. "You were amazing today. It was a privilege to watch." He held up his near-empty glass. "Are you going to come in and get a refill?"

"I'll just stand out here another minute, thanks." I wanted to be alone for a moment so I could run the day over in my mind again. There was so much to reflect on.

7   ENTER THE DRAGON

Savoring the past too much can be unhealthy, I discovered. Hanging on to past glories was just another way of not dealing with the present. Two weeks after Digby Wallace handed me the greatest bonanza of my lifetime, and one week after I had returned home, I was still closeting myself away in my home office as often as possible and, like a naughty boy stealing cookies, sneaking back into the memories of that incredible day. It was my way of dealing with the pain I was experiencing in my relationship with my wife, Kirsten. After coming home expecting a conquering emperor's welcome, I was confounded to find that her attitude toward me was even frostier than before I had gone away. She showed no sign of being happy for the success of my business trip and zero enthusiasm at the prospect of a more financially abundant future. Most hurtful of all was her disinterest in hearing about the magic principles I so passionately believed could at last make our country dream a reality. Things were really bad between us now. My worst nightmare, that I would destroy what I loved by trying to save it, seemed to be on the verge of materializing.

Like a regular addiction, my habit of escaping into my memories soon began affecting my ability to work and be with my family. I wondered how I would snap myself out of it and give my attention back to the things that needed taking care of. The answer was not long in coming.

Early one morning, only minutes after I'd stepped into my office to begin another day's work, the phone rang. I didn't get many incoming calls because of the proactive nature of my business, but when I did they were usually good news — excited clients eager to get some service going right away. Anyone with a problem tended to fax or email me. I picked up the phone and called out, "Good morning!" in that unnaturally cheerful tone that characters in children's TV shows greet each other with.

"Hello, Svengali," said a very alluring voice on the other end.

"Who's that?" The reference to my Bull Market nickname had completely thrown me. I'd been psyched up for business.

"Forgotten me already?" the disappointed voice admonished.

"Jilly, is that you?" Her voice sounded different over the phone. "How did you get my number?"

"Directory assistance, dummy," she said with an edge of malice, and then reverted to her little-girl-scorned voice.

"Wasn't I meant to call you, now that you're back with your wifey?"

I was bewildered by the tone she was using and the tack she was taking. "No, glad to hear from you, Jilly," I spluttered. "Just surprised, that's all."

There was a silence, then a venomous response. "Oh, so you're surprised, are you? I help you get a year's worth of business in one day, and then you conveniently forget about me, like I'm some kind of disposable prop."

I was at a loss for words. After another horrible silence, Jilly started up again with her bizarre incrimination. "You know, I've been waiting for you to call. I would have thought that was the least any self-respecting, half-decent human being would have done. Every single person I've talked to agrees that the right thing for you to do would have been to look after me once you got that business from Digby. I mean, we were partners. You would never have won that business if it weren't for me. But you didn't even think to thank me.

"You know, the whole night we didn't hear the end of it. You going on about what an amazing creator you were and how you'd just made a year's salary in one day. Boring Melissa Matheson to death by raving on about how to create by magic. And it never occurred to you that it all happened because of me. I started the party in the Bull Market; Digby invited you on his boat because he wanted me there, and I agreed to go for your sake; and I brought you around when you were about to crash out from alcohol poisoning.

If it hadn't been for me, you'd have walked out of the Bull Market the same little mouse you walked in as, not the arrogant, selfish prick you turned into."

I was mortified to think what an insufferable bore I must have been the night of Digby's party. A flush of shame singed my ears at the thought that I would presume to teach Melissa Matheson anything, especially considering she herself had just picked up a check that night for about twenty times what I earned in a year. I was embarrassed about all that, yet I couldn't relate to Jilly's claim to being a partner in my good fortune. "Why are you being like this, Jilly?" I pleaded with her.

"I just want what's mine," she said belligerently.

"But, Jilly," I said, trying to reason with her, "it's not like we made a deal. We were just having fun. I mean, you had a lot of fun, didn't you? I just happened to get permission to do business with Continental. It's not like Digby gave me a check or something. I still have to go in and sell the goods. I just got permission, that's all."

"But that's all you needed, wasn't it?" Jilly ranted. "You have to pass the hat around, that's all. But at the end of the day, there's going to be a year's pay in the hat. That's what you told everyone: it's in the bag. And I want my share." Her voice sounded as though she was just about to cry. "Half of that money is mine," she whined.

"What?" I croaked in astonishment. A warning bell was sounding in my brain. I knew I had to put Jilly straight right away. "You must be joking, Jilly," I said. "There's no way

half of that money is yours. Be reasonable. We're not partners. We didn't have any agreement. You were really good
to me, and I've thanked you for that, and I thank you again.
But to think that you have a right to half the money I make
because you were there, that's crazy. By that logic I'd have
to give Trevor half as well. He took me to the Bull Market."

"So I'm being unreasonable?" Jilly's voice sounded
contrite.

"Well, not unreasonable," I said as tactfully as possible.
"Just, well, maybe you misread the reality of the situation.
But you did help me."

"It's silly of me to ask for half, isn't it?" she said, as if
her demand were all water under the bridge.

"It was silly of me to misrepresent the deal with Digby.
Maybe if he had given me a bag of money, you would be
entitled to some of it. You and Trevor." All the time I was
speaking, I was wondering why I couldn't keep my stupid
mouth shut.

"So how's your wife?" Jilly came back pleasantly.

"Fine," I said as happily as when I'd picked up the
phone. I thought I was off the hook.

"Tell her about your visit to the Bull Market while you
were in town?" Jilly maintained the sweetly innocent tone
of voice.

"No," I admitted after some hesitation.

"What about the party on Digby's boat?"

"No," I said guardedly. I had a sickening suspicion of
where this new tack was going.

"So you wouldn't have told her about staying the night at my place, then?" The voice was still sweet, but far from innocent.

"No," I said, growing impatient with her. "I told you before, I don't want her to think that I'm out there galli-vanting about while she's stuck at home in the country. I don't want her to get the wrong idea."

"So what would happen if she found out?" Now the voice had lost its sweetness.

"I'm sure she'd feel like she got the raw end of the deal, which is why I don't think she needs to know." I didn't bother concealing my irritation.

"So what would happen if she found out that you'd slept with me?" The voice was full of sly curiosity.

"But, Jilly," I said, now totally on the back foot again, "we didn't do anything. I passed out at your place. You put me in your bed."

"But your wife doesn't know that, does she? I've got a Polaroid of me sitting on your lap at the Bull Market — the one you left with me, presumably because you didn't want your wife to see it. It's got the time and date on it. Then there's one of you and me arm in arm drinking champagne in a limo the same evening; a couple more on a yacht; some more back at my place; and the coup de grâce, you and me smiling from under the sheets the next morning. Looks like a pattern, doesn't it?"

"But we didn't do anything," I protested.

"But that's not what it looks like," Jilly sang out with a sick satisfaction. "You know, when a marriage is as shaky as yours, it only takes a single straw to break the camel's back."

"So what are you going to do?" I snapped. "Blackmail me?"

"Why, yes, that's exactly what I'm going to do," she laughed. "You know, I only wanted half, but because you're such a greedy pig, I'm going to insist on the whole lot. From what I've figured about your business, I'll give you three months to pay me what you told everyone you earned in a year. One third in a month's time, and another two payments a month apart after that."

"Wait a moment!" I cried. "Jilly, I thought we were friends. Look, it would take me six months to take all those orders and get paid for them. Then I'd have to pay tax on that money. Paying someone a year's salary would cost me a year and a half's work. I can't do it. Come on, don't do this to me."

"You're a sucker," she laughed again. "There's no question about whether you'll pay or not. The only question is how much. And that's not negotiable. I'll be in touch for the first installment." Her voice filled with an icy malevolence. "And if you don't have the money for me . . . to tell you the truth, I'd rather see you go to hell than get paid myself. I pity your wife, married to a weak bastard like you."

In my mind, I was thrashing about for a straw to clutch onto. "Jilly," I entreated, "what if I come back to town and we get together with Trevor and work out something fair we can all agree on? Come on, Jilly, we're friends, aren't we?"

"I thought so, but you're just a user, man. I want that

money just like I said, or your wife is going to find out about the hot week you and I spent together."

"What hot week? Jilly..."

But Jilly wasn't listening. "See you later, Svengali." She pronounced my nickname as sarcastically as she could. The line went dead.

I felt hollow, as if a vacuum had sucked every bit of substance out of me. I had an overwhelming sense of being an empty shell that was about to be flattened under the weight of a blind malevolence rolling relentlessly through the universe. It was the most comprehensive sense of disempowerment I could ever have imagined. Any notion that I had it in me to fly in the face of adversity and create whatever fantastic results I desired had flown right out the window. I remembered being in a motorbike accident many years earlier and looking down and seeing a jagged piece of femur sticking through my jeans. Not even the shock and panic I'd felt back then compared to the horror that gripped me now.

But then, deep within the mass of jelly I had turned into, I could feel an irrepressible part of me spring to life. It was my instinctive desperation, the adrenaline-charged aspect of the self designed to do absolutely anything to survive. With a hand shaking out of control, I found myself dialing a familiar number.

"Schroeder Benson Capital. How may I help you?" a perky voice chimed down the line.

"Get me Kaye Lerner, please," I snapped irritably.

"I'm afraid Ms. Lerner's unavailable at the moment. Can I take a message, sir?"

"Now listen here," I exploded. "My name is Mark Vale. I know exactly what meeting she's in, and I know it's not important. I'm calling on the most urgent business of her life. You get her on this line right now, or you're going to live to regret it."

I spent an anxious fifteen seconds drumming my fingers manically on my desk before Kaye's voice came on the line. "Kaye Lerner, Capital Markets."

"Kaye, thank God," I gasped with relief.

"Mark, what the hell's going on? You know better than to intimidate my receptionist and pull me out of my daily strategy session."

"Kaye, this is life or death. Put me on hold and pick up somewhere you can talk." When she came back on the line half a minute later, I told her my problem with the desperate clarity of someone talking his way out of a lynching.

"My God!" said Kaye once I'd finished. I could sense her absorbing everything I'd told her. After a while the logical solution occurred to her. "Why don't you just tell Kirsten?" she asked.

"How can I tell her now?" I cried in exasperation. "Can't you see, it's too late. Can't you see what it looks like, since I never told her anything to begin with? I'm telling you, Kaye, it'll be the end of our relationship. I won't see my kids again. I'll lose everything. You don't know the thread I'm hanging by here. When I came home, she didn't give a damn about the Continental deal. She didn't give a damn about all the magic I'd learned or my enthusiasm for the future. She's colder now than before I went away. I'm walking around on eggshells here. All I need is one foot out of place and it's all going to go to hell."

"What a mess," said Kaye absently. Then, as an afterthought she said, "You didn't do it, did you?"

"God, Kaye, of course I didn't. We just ended up at her apartment with Trevor and Melissa Matheson and a few people after Digby's party. I guess all the drinks from that night finally caught up with me. Before I knew it, Trevor was there in the morning to take me back to Cliff's. Him and his ridiculous Polaroid camera." Suddenly all the things I should have done to avoid my predicament occurred to me in a rush of bitter self-recrimination. I swore loudly to vent my frustration and anger. "What the hell am I going to do? I mean, do I go to the police? Do I call Trevor? Could he be in on it?"

"Don't be absurd, Mark," said Kaye sternly.

"Well, you know, she did this voodoo healing trick on me, and he seemed to know her very well." Pieces of the puzzle began coming together as I spoke. My theory seemed plausible to me. "It seems calculated, having a camera there every step of the way. Isn't it a bit of a coincidence that she's using the photos he took to blackmail me?"

"Get a grip on yourself, Mark." The way she said it, I could picture Kaye rolling her eyes in exasperation. "Trevor's always taking Polaroids. It's his way of initiating fun. He just isn't a con man. He doesn't need the money. And besides, why would he do so much to empower you and then rip you off? As for this Jilly woman, she'd have picked up a few tricks to sober people up, working in bars and saloons. Just face it, she's a good-time girl who saw her chance and took it. That's what you have to expect in that dog-eat-dog world she hangs around in."

"So what about the police?" I said, reaching desperately for a solution.

"That's not going to get you anywhere," Kaye said. "You have no proof she said any of this, and anyway, they would get Kirsten involved. One way or another, it will all come out if you go down that path." She paused, and then, in a voice that sounded like it hurt her to say it, she said, "I'm telling you, Mark, the best thing to do is tell Kirsten."

"I can't do that, Kaye." My voice cracked and my eyes flooded with tears. The anguish that ripped through me was a pain that reached beyond my flesh and clawed into my very soul. There was nothing I feared more than the dull, lifeless tone with which Kirsten had come to respond to my overtures of conciliation. It was unthinkable to unleash her loathing by burdening her with my sordid predicament. "What if I taped her repeating her threats?" I wondered out loud.

"Yeah . . . that might work," Kaye said dubiously.

"That's it!" I cried, seeing a bright light on the horizon for the first time. "That's it, Kaye. I've got to go. Sorry to trouble you."

I wasn't at all sorry. I was too involved in saving my own skin to worry about anyone else. I slammed the phone down and began rummaging through my briefcase for the scrap of paper I'd written Jilly's phone number on. It took me two searches to find it, and once I did I began organizing the recording device that attached to my telephone receiver, something I used to do to record calls for my sales coach to critique.

I shivered with excitement. In my mind, I was convinced I was going to nail Jilly right then and there, and the thought of turning the tables on her gave me a predator's bloodlust. The way I saw it, the windfall Digby Wallace had given me was not only the solution to my problems; it was also the ticket to my dreams. I felt morally justified in destroying anyone who tried to take that ticket away from me, and even a sense of pleasure at the prospect of doing so.

Trembling with a mixture of aggression and fear, I dialed Jilly's number and waited with bated breath for her to pick up the phone. My heart sank as a recorded message began playing at the other end. I was just about to hang up dejectedly when her voice cut in, singing out breathlessly, "Don't hang up, I'm here."

All my bravado deserted me as soon as I faced the reality of confronting her personally. The only thing I could do was swallow feebly. But the adrenaline-charged resolve within me wasn't going to let me back off. It prodded me to step into the ring. "Hi, Jilly. It's me," I croaked in a brittle voice.

"Oh, what do you want?" her voice changed from eager anticipation to sullen hostility.

"Look, Jilly," I tried to humor her, "your call earlier was such a surprise, I just wanted to see if I couldn't clear some things up. I realize that what I did . . . how I behaved . . ."

"What do you want? I'm in a hurry," she snapped.

"Jilly, please tell me," I tried my most ingratiating tone, "were you serious when you said you'd tell my wife we'd been together if I didn't give you all the money I earned from Continental?"

"No, Mark, I'd never say that," she said, flipping into her sweet-little-girl voice. "That would be blackmail. I just asked you to pay me the money you owe me, that's all. I'd never tell your wife you'd been with me, because that would be the end of your marriage; and I won't tell the police you forced yourself on me, because, even if I couldn't prove it, if word got out in the Bull Market about that you'd lose all your clients. I don't want you to lose your family and your means of earning a living. I know you've been out of the money markets too long to go back to them. All I want is my money."

Jilly was too street-smart for me. Not only had she avoided incriminating herself, she'd managed to escalate the consequences I'd suffer if I didn't pay her. Now what she was implying was that, even if I did come clean with my wife, she could still destroy my professional reputation. I hung up on her, feeling more dejected than ever.

I called Kaye straight back. Suspecting I wouldn't be long, she'd waited for my call rather than going back into her morning briefing. "It didn't work," I said miserably.

"Damn," Kaye empathized.

I don't know what I'd expected from Kaye, but it was more than "damn." I was angry with her for not being able to do anything other than suggest I make a clean breast of it to my wife. I wanted to punish her for not having the power to make my problem go away. "I'll have to come down and sort it out myself," I said despondently, hoping she'd interpret my decision as some sort of failure on her part.

"What do you expect to achieve by that?" said Kaye.

"I'll fix her." I wasn't joking, either. Trevor had been quite right to cast me as a flight-based personality type. What his assessment didn't recognize, however, was that when cornered, I never submitted — in fact, I became more aggressive than the most vicious, fight-based personality. As far as I was concerned, coming clean with my wife was death. The only hope I saw was in getting at Jilly somehow. Now that I was cornered, I was ready to fight her to the bitter end.

"Big mistake, Mark," Kaye said. "Reacting to this situation is only going to make it worse. You don't want to stir things up down here. You've got a month to figure this out. Sleeping on it for a night isn't going to harm you."

I was in a nasty mood. I wanted someone to pay for the horrible situation I was in, and I didn't mind if it was the person I'd turned to for help. "Are you mad?" I dragged my vowels out, sounding as contemptuous as I could. "How on earth do you think I'm going to sleep with this hanging over my head? Do you have any idea what it's like to have someone hold your whole life for ransom? Everything you worked for all your life? Your flesh and blood? Your soul mate? No way, Kaye! I'm coming back, and I'm going to take down whoever I need to."

My hysterical outburst had the desired effect on Kaye. "Okay, okay, Mark," she said. "I'll help you get out of this, but you have to stay put. Don't do anything rash. I'll fly up on Friday night, and we'll work something out."

"What are you going to be able to do?" I asked.

"Whatever I have to, Mark, whatever I have to," Kaye replied. "Just sit tight till Friday night, and I'll come up there and we'll sort this mess out. I promise you."

I was glad to have enrolled an ally in my misery, but I was loath to let her persuade me too easily. I didn't say anything.

"Okay? Will you just stay put and not do anything rash? Mark? Talk to me," she coaxed.

Finally, after an appropriate length of sullen silence, I relented. "Okay," I said in the most morose tone I could muster, "I'll stay put till the weekend."

When I was bitten by the Gibbons burrowing adder almost thirty years before, it took a while before the poison took effect and the pain set in. Believing I'd just picked up a mole snake, I'd thought nothing of the bite. That's what it was like after I put the phone down. I thought I'd be okay waiting till the weekend. I assumed that having a heavy hitter like Kaye on my side would let my mind rest easy. She was, after all, the associate director of a bank and an advisor to governments and huge corporations — a well-connected woman of influence used to playing hardball.

But that's assumptions for you! What actually happened was that, without anyone around to serve as a foil for my indignation, my mind inevitably began to fill with doubts. The first thought to occur to me was the depressing idea that Jilly didn't like me. I began to wonder whether she had a point about deserving a lot of the credit for my success with Digby. The more I thought about it, the more I could see she'd been a vital factor in the events that had led me to securing Continental's business. From there, I started to see myself the way Jilly must have seen me — as a miserly, mean-spirited, ungrateful bum. I felt really bad.

As if the pain of being despised by someone I liked and admired wasn't bad enough, I began to imagine the story of my sociopathic behavior spreading through the Bull Market. I squirmed to think that most probably by now Stavros and Digby and Trevor and Karen and maybe even Melissa Matheson had all been filled in as to what a cad I was. My heart sank as I pictured the hostile reception I'd get if I ever showed my face in their world again. All I could do was wring my hands and curse myself for ruining everything with my own selfishness and greed.

I thought of calling Trevor to explain my side of the story to him — why I should be excused for not thinking of or agreeing to pay Jilly her due. No sooner had I thought that than I became enraged again by the injustice of Jilly's demand. Hadn't Kaye, by virtue of her undertaking to help me in my fight against Jilly, acknowledged that Jilly's claim was nothing more than vulgar opportunism? Where did it say that proximity was any basis for a share of financial gain? How many times had people made deals on the basis of introductions I had given them? And had any of them ever offered me a cut? That's not how it worked. They returned the favor some day. They owed you one. That's how it worked. But using Jilly's logic, I should have charged an introduction fee to those of my friends who had met their husbands and wives through me.

I couldn't believe I'd put Jilly on such a pedestal. I despised myself for having been in awe of a two-bit hustler. Behind that facade of grace and charm and physical perfection lived a cunning scavenger forever on the lookout for someone's weakness to feed off. And what about Trevor? No matter how much Kaye vouched for him, I still couldn't help but suspect him of some involvement. He and Jilly were too close; everything had come together too smoothly; he and his camera had been everywhere. I was such an idiot. All the time I was fantasizing about being inducted into the magicians' inner circle, I was actually being set up for the sting of the century.

Within about thirty seconds, I'd come up with a conspiracy theory linking Trevor, Jilly, Digby, and Stavros to a worldwide web of evil that included the CIA, Middle Eastern terrorists, Zionist bankers, and Freemasons, if they still existed. Therein lay the source of my pain — the idea that Jilly was connected to, and had the support of, the city's most powerful businessmen, gangsters, and socialites. Comparing my own standing to what I imagined hers to be gave me an infuriating sense of helplessness.

And that's the vicious little circle my mind kept racing around for the next three days and nights. Going from feeling guilty and remorseful one moment to angry and ready to kill the next. One minute I was full of hope and could see all the factors in my favor, and the next minute I would swing back to despairing at the weight of circumstances aligned against me.

At the end of the argument, no matter which way I cut it, everything came down to the fact that if there were any kind of open fight about this, my wife would find out and all would be lost. And if I paid Jilly, all would be lost anyway. The solution lay in either talking or frightening her out of her hostile action. I couldn't see how I had the power to do either, even with Kaye on my side.

One would think my mind would have just given up and waited to see what unfolded once Kaye arrived, but not this little brain. Like a rat on a treadmill, it just kept going, repeating the cycle of soul-searching over and over again, never ceasing to hunt for some avenue of hope it might have overlooked the first hundred times around. But I just kept finding more and more reasons to be pessimistic, and my stress and anxiety intensified.

By the time Kaye arrived from the airport in her rental car on Friday night, I was a wreck. She didn't get a good look at me until we got to the guest cottage with her bags. When I turned on the lights inside the little hallway, the sight of me made her gasp with fright. She brought her hand up to her mouth in shock. "My God, Mark, you're a mess!" she exclaimed.

I carried her case through to the bedroom and sank down onto the bed. Looking up at her with what must have been the most pitiful expression she'd ever seen, I gave voice to my pent-up misery. "What do you expect?" I moaned, "I haven't slept for three days or nights. I haven't shaved or showered. I can't do anything except worry about this. I've got clients waiting for me to take big orders from them, but I can't even call them. I'm afraid that if I put my attention on something else, even for a second, something really vital to this nightmare is going to elude me. That's what it is, Kaye, a waking nightmare. I feel like I've been hung out to dry on an electric fence."

"That's terrible, Mark." Kaye sat down on the bed next to me and put an arm around my shoulders. I had somehow assumed that once Kaye arrived I'd feel better, but now, even in her embrace, I felt nothing but bleak despair. "What about Kirsten?" she asked.

"I don't know," I replied, not sure what Kaye was asking me. I was vaguely aware that her question had triggered some emotions deep inside me, but my mind was too numb to register what they were. "I don't know. I just can't be around her or the kids. It brings up too much pain in me. I hate myself for being such a loser, for not being good enough to hold together what I love."

"Has she said anything, though?" Kaye pressed me.

"No," I said, "I think she's relieved not to have to deal with what's happening between us." I wished I could cry and stop the awful sensation of my mind being stretched as taut as a drum skin. But the relentless desperation within me wouldn't let go. It was going to hang on to the pretense that nothing was lost till the bitter end. It wasn't going anywhere near the suggestion that it was all over.

"You know what I wish, Kaye?" I sighed. "I wish I'd studied medicine or law, or something else with some kind of security, something with a consistently high income."

"Come on, Mark, you're just torturing yourself now," said Kaye in dismay.

"I know, but that's what it is — it's torture. That's why I've got to sort this mess out. It's driving me mad." I turned to face her. "What are we going to do, Kaye? What are we going to do?" I implored.

Kaye dropped her arm off my shoulder and sighed a heavy sigh. "Well, we can't do anything until you've had a good sleep. We can't talk about anything while you're in this state."

"So how am I supposed to get out of this state?" I responded testily. "The only thing that's going to get me out of this state is knowing that this nightmare is going to go away."

"Well, it's not!" said Kaye. "You think that your state of mind is going to change when your problem changes. But it's not. Your problem is going to change when your state of mind changes."

"So how do I do that?" I asked in bewilderment.

"I'm going to teach you a meditation technique," replied Kaye calmly. "Do you want to hear it?" I had become used to pushing Kaye around, but now her tone and bearing conveyed a powerful sense of authority I found impossible to defy.

"Sure," I said.

"Okay, so here's what you do," said Kaye. "You lie down on your bed and close your eyes, and you imagine God is going to appear to you."

I was waiting for her to tell me the actual technique, but she didn't say anything else. After a while I had to ask her, "So what's the technique?"

"That's it!" she replied. "You lie there and you keep imagining God is going to appear."

"Then what happens?" I asked dubiously.

"Well, then God will come to you and your state of mind will change," said Kaye in the most matter-of-fact way.

"What if I don't believe in God?" I countered.

"That doesn't matter," Kaye sang out. "This meditation doesn't depend on belief; it depends on imagination. You just imagine that a higher power or force is coming to visit you. The only thing that's important is that you keep imagining it's going to happen, no matter what."

Kaye's proposition was probably the most outrageous thing anyone had ever suggested to me. The idea that God would reach down to ease my troubled mind was absurd, yet something in Kaye's affirmative manner made me buy it. Perhaps it was because I was so desperate for something to believe in. All I know is that the thought of trying her technique actually brightened me up.

BACK AT THE MAIN HOUSE, I excused myself as early as I could and went to bed after a quick shower. As I rested my head on the pillow, I became aware for the first time just how tense and nervous I was feeling. A deep grief seemed to emanate from my chest. I found it hard to breathe for fear of giving life to that unbearable sadness. Mixed in with the dull ache of the grief were short, stabbing pains I came to recognize as spasms of self-loathing kicking at my heart. Meanwhile, my mind felt like it was being strangled while looking out on an endless, lifeless expanse of wasteland. It didn't matter whether Kaye's meditation worked or not; the only bit of comfort I had was imagining that something miraculous could happen to absolve me of my pain. I closed my eyes and imagined that God's arrival was imminent. For some reason, I pictured a knight in black armor riding up in a fanfare of bugles and trumpets. I didn't think it was the right image, but hard as I tried I couldn't shake it.

Right from the beginning I never really expected anything to happen. Still, I couldn't stop myself from acting as if something would. Once I had entered my little make-believe world, the expectation wouldn't let me go. I was stuck there feeling as if something phenomenal was just about to happen.

I'd been lying there for perhaps five minutes when my doubt got the better of me. I was just beginning to think to myself that waiting for a knight in armor was ridiculous, when it suddenly occurred to me that something was different. But rather than perceiving a presence I'd expected, I felt as if something was missing.

Hard as I tried to go back to the positive expectation Kaye had insisted was the key to her meditation, I couldn't stop myself from wondering what was missing. Then it dawned on me. I didn't have my tension headache any longer. My mind was empty and calm. I remembered the pain in my chest, but when I checked in on it, it too had disappeared. The crushing weight had lifted, and I was breathing normally. A thrill of mild euphoria tingled my spine as I realized something had happened. The technique was working. Then a sudden twinge of panic gripped me.

Something was telling me that this wasn't the end result; this was only the beginning. This was the calm before the storm. Someone was coming.

And then it happened. The knight in black armor came galloping through the wall of my bedroom. I jumped up in fright, surprised to see that there was nothing there. But when I lay back down on the bed, I felt as though I were floating in the air. It wasn't even me in my body. I had been taken over by an energy of pure delight. I was an innocent, carefree spirit nestled in the loving embrace of the most benevolent, all-encompassing presence imaginable — not that I could ever have imagined such a sense of acceptance, love, and protection. I could feel myself grinning from ear to ear. Thrill after thrill danced through my body, as a celestial noise more beautiful than any music I had ever heard floated in my head.

As an experiment, I tried to reflect on the dramas in my life. I couldn't. They were nothing I could even remotely relate to. The magnetic force of the bliss surrounding me was too potent to let me be affected by such petty issues. I fell asleep feeling a sense of complete protection. My last thoughts were: "So, this is my real mother; this is my true father."

8 LOSING FAITH

The first memories I had of life came simply from the wonder with which I beheld the world. Living in the wilds of Africa as my family did, we had a home and garden that hosted a whole menagerie of animals, including hunting dogs, cats, peacocks, goats, and rabbits, as well as orphaned gazelles, zebras, leopards, warthogs, monkeys, and baboons. Life was so full of magic I almost couldn't bear it. Every day, about an hour before dawn, a euphoric current would run through me like an alarm clock, and I'd sit bolt upright in my bed, wondering what adventures lay in store for me that day. Would the thirty-foot python still be lying coiled around the roots of the big fig tree down by the river, patiently digesting the bush pig he'd swallowed two months ago? Would the gardeners find canaries chilled by the cold winter's night lying on the road and thaw them out beside the stove for me to let fly into the first rays of sunlight? Would I lie on my back looking up at the azure sky, watching dandelion-seed parachutes drifting surrealistically off into another world?

The anticipation of the wonder that awaited me would be too great for me to lie in until it was light. I'd bound out of bed and run outside into the eerie death of night, a thrill coursing through my body as I tore about, naked, across the endless expanse of lawn. One by one, the adolescent animals would shake themselves out of their nocturnal stupor and race over to join me in frolicking around the garden, all of us feeding off each other's exhilaration. Unaware of our future roles as either predators or prey, we'd prance about together, innocently celebrating the wonder of the world. I'd never forgotten how I always ended up at the bottom of the garden, standing there surrounded by snuffling creatures of every description keeping me company as I stared up at the predawn sky in amazement, my mouth agape at the pail of phosphorescent milk spilled across the heavens, and the stars like white hot embers glowing in a bed of black velvet. It was as if the stars were some kind of ethereal life-form communicating in twinkles and glints and winks. Sometimes it felt as if they were all talking to me, and I'd get the feeling that if I didn't close my eyes to the magic about me I'd explode. All I could do to stop myself from bursting was begin rampaging around the garden again.

Waking up the morning after trying out Kaye's sublime meditation technique, I felt as close as I'd ever come to recapturing that sense of childhood bliss. Certainly the same degree of vitality and the zest for life I'd had as a child were missing, but there was the feeling that life was an endless series of gifts waiting to be bestowed. Looking out from my bedroom window at the first rays of sun filtering through the trees, and beyond to the cows grazing in the valley below, I had a pleasant sense that everything was as it should be and that the world was a stage that had been set for something wonderful to happen at any moment. The only thing missing, thankfully, was the queue of worries that normally insisted they be taken care of. Right then, in that moment, life wasn't something that required a lot of work; it was something to enjoy.

For the first time in years, I felt at home in my own home. As my children chattered away at the breakfast table, telling me about the lifetime they had lived in the last couple of hours, I felt like their legitimate father and they felt like my children. We were there, connected, living together on the same side of the water, not separated by the gulf of my fear that they could slip from my grasp at any time.

And it was the same with Kirsten. I felt like her man, her lover, her friend, and she felt like my soul mate, as close and familiar and connected as if we'd been together since the beginning of time. There was an ease and a playfulness and a lovingness in her that morning that reminded me of all the reasons why I loved her and all the beauty I had ever seen in her.

The sun was shining. The grass was singing. The bacon and eggs tasted wonderful. My family was happy. My wife did love me. We did live in the most beautiful place on earth. Everything was perfect. This life was so charmed.

And that was the problem. The more clearly I could see the brilliance of the life I'd made for myself, the more anxious I began to feel about holding it together. The peace and contentment I felt on waking had highlighted all the blessings I should be grateful for, but in the end those blessings became a stark reminder of all I stood to lose.

It was as if fate were dangling my blessed life in front of my eyes, reminding me that there was no room for complacency, that there were reasons to remain vigilant, things to secure, things to take care of. This charmed life couldn't be freely enjoyed yet; there were many unknowns to be worked out, many pitfalls to be avoided, and one huge problem to be resolved.

And so the scales in my mind slowly tipped from high-spirited exaltation to ponderous anxiety. The day seemed to lose its freshness early on, and shortly after breakfast I was already unable to hold my attention on my family. Even as my kids climbed all over me on the lawn, all I could think of was the business I had neglected over the last few days and the plan of action Kaye might come up with to counter Jilly's ambush.

I was dying to get together with Kaye to formulate a viable strategy for dealing with the killer problem at hand, but she'd disappeared in her rental car before either Kirsten or I had gotten up. I didn't know where she was. Before anyone could notice how agitated I was and take it personally, I made some excuse about nonexistent information that had to be sent to a client and hurried off to my office, where I could fret in private.

Mercifully, Kaye wasn't long in getting back to the farm. I didn't think I could take another minute of feeling as if my emotional body were being pulled around like a carcass on the savannah. "What are you doing here?" cried Kaye as she burst into my office, an accusing look on her face.

"Just sending some stuff off to a publisher," I replied, pretending to look through the pile of paperwork sitting in my in-tray.

"Nonsense," said Kaye disdainfully. "Oh, come on, Mark. It's the weekend. You should be spending time with your family. What's wrong with you?"

"Bloody hell, Kaye," I exclaimed, letting go of all pretenses, "you know what's going on. How am I supposed to hang out with my family when I'm sick with worry? I don't want to bring them down, too. Besides, how could I explain what's going on? What would I tell Kirsten?"

Kaye had perched on the armrest of the sofa across from my desk. She fixed me with a pitiless look and in a disgusted tone of voice said, "Well, you could try telling her the truth."

"Give me a break, Kaye," I squealed, taken aback by her hostility. "Whose side are you on?"

"I'm not on anyone's side, Mark," said Kaye, her tone softening. "I'm here to serve everyone's best interests."

"What are you talking about?" I responded. "You're either on my side or Jilly's. There's no mutual ground in this thing."

"Oh, Jilly," said Kaye absently. "I'm not thinking about her. There's nothing I can do about her."

"What are you saying?" I cried, feeling as if Kaye had just pulled the plug on my life. "That's what you're here for, isn't it? To help me?"

"I am here to help you, yes," Kaye said evenly, "but I can't do anything about your problem."

"Kaye, are you messing with my mind?" I howled. "On the phone you said you'd come up here and sort this thing out."

Kaye looked at me dispassionately. "I did fly all the way up here to sort this thing out. And I will. I just can't help you with your problem."

"You can't help me?" I was stunned.

"No, problems can't be solved, Mark. I know you expect me to come up with some magical solution to Jilly, but I can't see how I can stop her. I haven't got any influence over her; I don't know anyone who does. You're either going to give her what she wants, or her accusation is going to make its way to Kirsten."

I now knew how it would feel if someone were to suck all the blood out of me in three seconds. "What do you mean, problems can't be solved?" I whimpered. "If that's the inevitable outcome, how are you helping me sort this out?"

"I can't take your problem away, Mark." The lack of emotion in Kaye's voice made it sound callous to my ears. "No one can. Problems are all in the mind. Anything you do to fix any problem in life only makes it worse."

"Look, Kaye, stop jerking me around," I snapped. "You have problems every day at work. Isn't that what you get paid for? To solve everyone's problems?"

"No, Mark, that's where you're wrong," said Kaye with maddening calmness. "I get paid to take people beyond their problems. That's where I can be of service to you."

I was speechless. For Kaye to have said she would help me sort this mess out and then turn around and say there was nothing we could do about Jilly didn't make any sense at all. If she hadn't been the only person I felt I could share this dilemma with, I would have told her to go to hell right then and there.

Kaye must have sensed she was skating on thin ice, because she softened her voice again. "What I can do," she said, "is enable you to see this whole situation in a new light. Maybe when you see things in this new light, you will realize you don't have a problem."

"But nothing you say is going to take away the fact that Jilly is blackmailing me, and that if I don't give her the money she's going to frame me," I said in my most acid tongue.

"That's not going to change," agreed Kaye gently. "And if you look for the solution in that fact changing, you're gone. You have to look beyond your problem for your solution."

"Meaning?" I demanded.

"I'll tell you something Trevor taught me," replied Kaye. "The first magicians of old used to maintain that everything in the world was a vibration. The sky, the earth, the ocean, the trees, our bodies, our mind, our thoughts and feelings, even our problems and solutions — everything is a vibration. And they used to say that you use the higher vibration against the lower vibration, which means — "

"Ah, please. Spare me the magic crap, Kaye," I snorted. "Don't you get it? That's what got me into this mess in the first place. Do me a favor — don't talk to me about magic. If that's what you've got to offer, I'd rather not know. Honestly."

"Well, what happened to you and all your talk about how you'd seen the light and how you were going to manifest this amazing, abundant lifestyle?" said Kaye, unperturbed. "Last time I saw you in the city, you were all fired up, telling me how there wasn't anything you couldn't do now that you'd discovered magic. What's happened? I mean, here's your chance. If ever there was an opportunity to apply what you learned from Steve and Trevor, this is it."

"I must have been deluded," I said, hoping to hurt her by denigrating her beliefs. "If you must know, I have been focusing on improving my relationship with Kirsten. Ever since I got back from town, and even before, I've been visualizing us reconnecting in the old, happy way we used to. But you know what? Things have gotten worse. Nobody told her it's supposed to work, that she's supposed to be chilling out."

Somehow I was cheered up by my own sarcasm. Perhaps it gave me some sense of power, the thought that I could put someone down. "You know," I sneered, "this magic crap is all well and good when it comes to tricks, but out here in the real world, where you're trying to survive, it doesn't cut any mustard, I can tell you."

"Well, that's your problem, Mark," said Kaye as calmly as ever. "You're trying to survive. And you know what? The way you're going, you're going to lose everything. You can try to make me feel bad, but guess what? I'm not the one who's going to lose his wife and kids, and farm, and friends, and every penny he's ever worked for. I'm not the one on the verge of being destroyed by his own stubbornness and narrow-mindedness."

Kaye might have shot me in the chest point-blank; that's how powerfully her words hit me. What she said blew the tracks I'd been running along to kingdom come. My will to fight her came to a grinding halt. Who was I kidding? I wasn't in charge of the situation. What was the point of acting like I was? I gaped at Kaye remorsefully.

"You know what the real problem here is?" she continued. "The real problem is that you're not focused on anything but yourself. You've been focusing on you and what you stand to lose. That's all you care about. You don't care about Kirsten or the kids. You're not doing anything for them. You're not thinking about them. It's just you and your welfare. If you really cared about the people in your life, you'd be interested in what I have to offer. You might not like the fact that magic doesn't give you power and control over everyone and everything, but it's the only thing that stands half a chance of stopping you from ruining everything for everyone."

I swallowed self-consciously, averting my eyes from her accusing stare. Though contrite and defeated, I was relieved to have had the stuffing knocked out of me. It dawned on me that the hell I had sunken into over the last week and a half must be the formidable test Trevor had predicted I would soon have to face. In my deflated state, I had to acknowledge that I had fallen into a downward spiral not because of bad luck, or because magic was bogus, or because Kirsten was a cold fish, or because I had been conned by Jilly or let down by Kaye, but, more than likely, because of some false value I was hanging on to. I had no idea of what it was or what I could do about it. Like a lost sheep following its shepherd home through the hills, I had a sense that Kaye knew the way out of this mess. Something told me that following her lead was the way to go.

"Look, Kaye, I'm sorry," I said, swallowing nervously again. "It's been a rough time. But don't get me wrong; I really appreciate your being here for me." Apologizing made me feel a lot better. A murmur of optimism rose up in me. Kaye did have a plan after all, just not the kind I had imagined. Even as my rational mind screamed its objection to giving up on solving the problem, I felt a sense of excitement at the thought of following an unknown path.

"Oh, look, it's okay, Mark," she sighed. "Losing faith is an inevitable step along the way when you're starting out." She stood up and jumped up and down on the spot two or three times. "Well, then," she said, rubbing her hands together, "let's go for a bike ride."

"A bike ride?" I exclaimed in horror. It was only then that I noticed she was wearing bicycle pants. "But we haven't ridden the bikes for ages," I protested. "The tires are flat."

"Well, that's what I've been doing this morning," Kaye smiled. "I've been into the village to get them pumped up. You go and change, and I'll clip the wheels back onto the bikes."

"I'll just have to see what the family's up to," I countered feebly.

"I just spoke to Kirsten before I came over here," said Kaye. "She's taking the kids to a women's gathering this morning."

It's strange she didn't tell me, I thought to myself. I wasn't sure what made me feel worse, the fact that Kirsten hadn't bothered to consult with me about her plan, or that I was being dragged out for a mountain bike ride on a hot summer morning.

9 FREEDOM

Pedaling into the hills behind our small holding was hard work in the midmorning heat, but once we were riding along the mountain ridges it was very pleasant. A mild breeze fanned our faces, and the canopy of overhanging branches shielded us from the fierce sun. Every now and then we'd come across a firebreak, and we'd be able to look out over the forest undulating down to the sea. As resistant as I'd been to the suggestion at first, I was truly happy Kaye had insisted we go riding. The physical exertion and the oxygen to the brain had restored the ease of mind and exhilaration I'd enjoyed before breakfast. I felt entirely amenable to whatever tack Kaye wanted to take. I rode up beside her. "When you said that problems can't be solved, what did you mean?"

"Sounds crazy, doesn't it?" laughed Kaye.

"It does," I panted, pedaling full steam to keep up with her. "I mean, if a river keeps flooding, that's a problem, isn't it? So then the government builds a levee. That solves the problem, doesn't it?"

"That's a good point," admitted Kaye. "But what happened in your example? What was the end result?"

"No more flooding?" I ventured.

"Well, that too," said Kaye. "But basically they changed the structure, didn't they?"

"I suppose so," I agreed lamely.

"Well, that's the thing, you see," Kaye began explaining. "Whatever you do to cope with the river flooding isn't going to stop the river from flooding. The government can bail out the flood victims, and everyone can build their houses on stilts, but in the long term that river is going to keep on wreaking havoc. The only solution is to change the structure. When the structure changes, the problem goes away. Coping with the flooding solves nothing. Changing the structure by building a levee eliminates the flood problem. That's what I was trying to tell you earlier. You see, magicians don't solve problems; they make them go away. That's real magic, isn't it? Making things vanish?"

Kaye began to laugh to herself. I wondered in amazement why she wasn't panting breathlessly like me. She'd pulled slightly ahead now and had to call out over her shoulder to carry on talking to me. "You don't want to be rearranging deck chairs on the *Titanic*; you want to be on another ship altogether. That's the difference between magicians and everyone else. Magicians know when to get off the sinking ship, while everyone else tries to keep it afloat."

I had to put in a superhuman effort to draw abreast of

her again. "I get your point," I wheezed, "but I don't see how it applies to my life." As soon as I said the words, I began dreading Kaye's response.

"There's a lookout just ahead," she said. "Let's have a rest up there."

We soon came across a small parking area on the side of the road and pulled off there. We leaned our bikes against one of the tables and walked along the pathway following a narrow finger of bald granite pointing out into a deep valley. Looking out to the east, we saw that the country opened up into rolling pasture bounded by a shimmering sea. About a mile to the west, where the valley came to a dead end, we could see the top half of a waterfall disappearing behind a tree-lined ridge.

"Wow, look at that, will you!" cried Kaye, leaning over the railing at the edge of the cliff. I put my head over the railing and looked down. It must have been about five hundred feet down to the valley floor. I felt a disturbing sensation, as if the granite walls wanted to suck me off the cliff top, and I imagined my fragile carcass being dashed against the rocks below. I retreated from the cliff edge feeling all woozy. No surprises there — I have a chronic fear of heights.

Kaye screamed out, "Geronimo!" and listened to her own cry reverberating around the valley. Then she turned around to look at me, her face alight with euphoria. "All those endorphins," she laughed. "Isn't life wonderful?"

We perched ourselves on a couple of large weathered boulders, and without any preamble Kaye began answering my question. Because she wasn't looking at me as she spoke, and because I was still feeling woozy, I didn't realize what she was talking about at first.

"Now, if we look at the structure in your life, it's like a city under siege. What happens to a city under siege? I'll tell you. The inhabitants begin to starve. Resources dry up. Everything becomes scarce. People's spirits sink. In the end, the only thing they have is the wall around them keeping them alive. But they have no life. And then they begin to fight with each other. They argue about who's wasting precious resources, who's not pulling their weight, who's not showing loyalty to the group, who's causing their problems.

"That's the inevitable outcome of the siege mentality. People under siege think only about how to preserve resources, how to shore up the defenses, how to keep up the fighting spirit. It doesn't occur to them to give up the siege. They'd rather live miserably than surrender. They can't accept surrender as a viable option. You're living under siege, Mark. That's the underlying structure of your life. And it's draining you of everything you love."

Kaye looked at me intently, as if to underscore the earnestness of her closing remark, but her words didn't affect me in the slightest. I couldn't relate to what she was saying. "What are you talking about, Kaye?" I said. "I'm out there in the world fighting for what I want. I'm not hiding."

"No?" said Kaye. "Then why can't you tell Kirsten about Jilly? How come you're afraid of an allegation that isn't even true? How come you won't make a stand for the truth?"

"Ah, well, that's different," I sputtered. "That's just an

isolated situation based on my circumstances at the moment. But when this is sorted out and we've got our finances on track and things are solid again, it'll be different. This is just a sensitive time, that's all."

"Yeah, but can't you see that it's never going to be different?" Kaye countered. "Can't you see that your circumstances are based on the underlying structure of your life, and that trying to respond to your circumstances is only going to reinforce the underlying structure? This is your flood, Mark. Do you think throwing some money at it and putting your house up on stilts is going to help?"

"You've lost me now, Kaye," I said dismissively.

"Well, let me come straight to the point." She waited for me to make eye contact before she went on. "What do you think you're trying to achieve in your life?"

"A great lifestyle for my family."

"Do you really believe that?"

"Of course. Why? What do you think?"

"It's not what I think, Mark," said Kaye, "it's what I know. And I'll tell you what you're doing. You're hiding. You've retreated from the world to stay safe."

"Rubbish!" I cut in.

"It's true," said Kaye, unfazed. "After Kirsten had the babies, she came into her power. She wasn't a little girl anymore. You see, she has talents, capabilities, powers, and desires that have come alive and that seek expression. They're going to take her out of your orbit and put her in her own orbit. She's not going to be so reliant on you emotionally, financially, socially, creatively, and so on.

You're terrified of that power. You don't believe you can survive her power. That's why you won't empower her with the truth now. You don't believe that if she's in touch with her own power she'll stick around. So you disempower her. You manipulate and control her. You keep the truth from her. You keep her locked in a mansion out in the country far away from other powerful, creative women, far away from where her talents can be employed.

"That's what's going on here, Mark. Your own insecurity is your underlying problem. You're living under siege. And your struggle to make your business work is your struggle to finance your siege. This is your false value. You're trying to prop up your siege, not support your real life or Kirsten's or your children's.

"That's why you're so cut up about magic. That's what happens at first to everyone who experiences magic: they want it to resolve their underlying problems, and they're always dismayed when magic won't do that. Because magic is a servant of the truth, you see. Once magic is employed, it begins corrupting the dysfunctional structure and pointing to the true structure. When people's natural abilities don't produce what they expect, they go deeper and deeper into their swing circles. Instead of allowing themselves to see what's going on, they tend to try to bulldoze their dysfunctional agendas through. If you think about it, that's the basis of all human suffering."

It sounded totally preposterous, absolutely absurd, straight out of left field, but at the same time I knew Kaye was right. The diamond bullet that Trevor had talked about exploding in his mind had just caught me between the eyes. A bell was ringing like mad in my head. I felt a mixture of awe, alarm, and humiliation all at the same time, though most of all I felt relief — relief that what was really wrong in my life had finally been named.

"But Kirsten wanted to move to the country as much as I did. How come it's all my fault?" I asked meekly, out of sheer curiosity, not resistance.

"Oh, it's not your fault, Mark," Kaye replied. "I'm not apportioning blame here. Kirsten will have to examine her motives herself. You've both made an unspoken pact to set up a safe little world where neither of you can be threatened. You've set up an inward-looking world where neither of you will be tempted to diverge from your merged reality. That's why you can't let on that you've been out there having fun. You've broken the agreement by exposing yourself to external temptation. But let's not blame or speculate. Let's just look at the obvious. I mean, do you relate to what I'm saying about you?"

I nodded my head in the affirmative, deep in thought.

"Good," said Kaye. "And what I'm saying about Kirsten is true, too. Why do you think she isn't happy about any financial success you have? It's because it's funding the siege, and she doesn't want to live under siege. She wants the siege to fail. Maybe not intellectually, but in her heart. She wants to be somewhere more socially dynamic, somewhere she can practice her artistic talents. Everyone knows Kirsten's a designer. With her talent, she should be at art college or studying architecture."

Kaye left it there. We sat in silence for a while, endur-
ing the midmorning sun that beat down on us. The stillness
was shattered by a piercing cry over the valley, and seconds
later an eagle came gliding past at eye level. Maybe it was
my imagination, but I fancied that the majestic bird eyed us
ponderous, land-bound creatures with disdain before lofting
into the sky on an updraft with an effortless twitch of its
wing tips.

"Why didn't I see what I was doing?" I wondered out
loud.

"Well," said Kaye, "our fear is so ingrained we hardly
ever notice that it's driving us. We just assume we're doing
the natural, logical thing. Like just now, when you moved
away from the railing, you were being stimulated by the idea
of being dashed against the rocks on the valley floor. There
was no actual likelihood of that happening, only the thought
of it. But nevertheless you automatically moved away till
you were far enough from the edge for that thought not to
occur to you. There was no conscious choice behind your
action. I think it's rare for people to see what their true motivations are, what's driving them. Their underlying structure is a few levels below their conscious awareness."

I wasn't daunted by what Kaye was saying. I was fas-
cinated. "So how are we supposed to know what our
true motivations are?" I asked out of genuine interest. "Or
are we doomed to the stimulus-response orientation, like
amoebas?"

"Not at all," laughed Kaye. "It's actually easy to see
your deeper motivations. Your deeper motivations form the

underlying structure of your consciousness, and it's useful to see that, because it's determining inevitable results."

"So, are you going to tell me what the secret is, or are you going to keep it to yourself?" I prompted Kaye light-heartedly, once again feeling the pleasure of talking about magic.

"First of all," Kaye responded, "you have to want to see. The reason you can't see is because you don't want to see; you've made a decision not to see. A long time ago, you created a swing circle. You decided what life was about, what was important, and what you would have to get together and hold together. You took control away from your natural ability and handed it over to the keeper of your swing circle, your rational mind. Your rational mind sees things only in terms of your swing circle. It believes that the underlying structure of your swing circle is the only valid structure — that whatever you've decided life is about must be what it's about. It doesn't entertain any other possibility. In your case, you absolutely take for granted the idea that life is about avoiding being abandoned. You don't even realize that you are constantly acting on this avoidance."

Kaye took a sip of water from her drink bottle and offered it to me. "So you see," she continued, "your focus creates reality. Whatever you decide the end result is determines your reality. You see everything in terms of that objective. In your case, you've decided that you're powerless, and that you've got to hoard what you have so you don't lose it. That's your objective, and your thoughts and feelings are all related to that objective. When that objective looks secure, you're up; and when it looks shaky, you're down.

"So then you're running around responding to your thoughts and feelings. They've become a paradigm for you, a little world you lose yourself in. They give you the impression that your security agenda is objective reality, is what life is actually about. It's tricky and insidious. You can no longer see that your thoughts and feelings are merely responses to the underlying structure, because that deeper motivation is now screened from view by those very thoughts and feelings."

Kaye was distracted by the piercing cry of the eagle. She looked up into the sky but didn't see it anywhere. "Goodbye to you, too," she called out toward the valley. Looking back at me, she said, "So there you are, in this virtual reality you've created for yourself; but you don't want to see that it's an illusion — that what's driving it might be dysfunctional — because it's your swing circle, the paradigm you've set up to maintain control. It's the life drama you play out in order to keep control. No one wants to see that their life is a myth of their own making, so they choose not to see. They keep their awareness confined to the dimension they're caught up in. It's a choice. And so, too, is seeing through your myth; it's a decision, an intention.

"Once you make the choice to reveal the myth, then you'll start seeing what's going on. The signs are always there. Life is always telling you; other people are always telling you. As soon as you make the choice, your conscious awareness will begin opening to what's really going on in your life. That's the first thing you have to do: decide!"

It seemed a bit too simple. There must have been something I'd missed. "That's it?" I said, searching her face for a sign of what she might be holding back.

"No," said Kaye. "That's only the start; you have to be willing. But ultimately your awareness is determined by the underlying structure in your consciousness. So, if you want to shift to a higher level of awareness, you're going to have to establish a higher structure in your consciousness. You use the higher against the lower."

"How do you do that?" I asked, relieved to hear there was something practical to be applied.

"Well," replied Kaye, "up until now you've been living out your illusion. You've been focused on your dysfunctional agenda. That's all you've been seeing. What you can do now is to begin focusing on your truth. It's time to establish the value of being true to yourself. That's the thing to focus on now; that's the vision to hold. When you do that, a whole new set of information will begin occurring to you."

Kaye had been talking in the most matter-of-fact way. There was nothing at all confrontational in her manner, and I had been following her enthusiastically. What she was saying now, though, made me uneasy. It was as though I were standing at the rail looking over the cliff again.

"So what are you supposed to do once you've seen all this stuff?" I complained sourly, fully aware that the remarks I was about to make were designed solely to resolve my uneasiness. "So Kirsten and I are hiding from the world in some way — how does that help me, or us? What are we supposed to do now? That doesn't help us get out of this situation. We still can't afford to move back to the city. Whatever we do, we're still going to need money."

"You and your bloody money!" laughed Kaye, totally unruffled by my outburst. "You see, that's the reality of your old agenda. Just look at what you're assuming. No, really! Instead of barking at me, just feel the pain that's coming up for you and tell me what you're assuming. What are you telling yourself?"

My first response was to begin arguing with Kaye, but she put her hand up and wouldn't let me say a thing. Sitting there with nowhere to go, all I could do was feel what I was feeling. As had happened when I was with Trevor, I was surprised at the relief I experienced surrendering to my emotions. Kaye watched my face soften.

"So, Mark, just feel what you're feeling and tell me: how are you defining yourself?"

"Well, as kind of inadequate," I said, searching for words. "Like I'm not good enough for people to like. It's as if I haven't got what it takes to be accepted by others."

"Okay," said Kaye softly. "What about others: how are you defining them?"

"I feel like they're somewhere else. Like they're interested in something that I haven't got." I didn't feel confident in expressing myself, but the sense of freedom and power I got from examining my own perception made it easy for me to oblige Kaye.

"So what you're saying is that there's nothing inherently attractive about you?" Kaye kept her voice neutral; there wasn't a hint of either sympathy or judgment. "As if, left to their own devices, people would naturally drift away from you. Like you're inherently separate from them. There's something you have to do to hold on to them. Is that it?"

"Exactly!" I cried, responding to the thrill of Kaye's words resonating in my body. What she said next resonated even more strongly, although I felt the words more as a sting than a buzz.

"So you have to manipulate them, don't you? You have to buy them."

"That's true," I admitted. In my mind, I could see a vision of myself without material trappings, and everyone leaving me like rats deserting a sinking ship.

"You see that picture in your mind now?" I heard Kaye calling to me from somewhere far away. I looked up to find her studying my face intently. "You see what you're thinking right now?"

I nodded.

"Well, you've just had the rare privilege of seeing what's driving you!" she cried. "That's what you're focusing on. That's your core value — the underlying structure. And you see that picture in your mind? That's the message your mind is giving itself. Under all the noise of your daily life, that's the picture your mind is constantly looking at. That's what it's creating. No matter how desperately you're earning money and working on being loved, the picture you've just seen is the message underlying all that striving."

I swallowed self-consciously, feeling a mixture of foolishness and alarm.

"Now if you look at your life," said Kaye gently, "you'll see that you're coming closer and closer every day to manifesting that picture. The harder you strive, the closer you get to having more of what you're trying to get away from. So you see, Mark, in answer to your question 'What do I do with this information?': awareness gives you a choice — the choice to carry on as you were or to create a new structure based on a set of values that will let you put yourself on a path to creating an abundance of what you actually love. It gives you the option of having a functional focus in life."

A sense of impending doom swept over me. I wasn't enjoying the conversation anymore. It seemed to me that the disaster I had unconsciously set up in my life was now a foregone conclusion. The picture of everyone abandoning me came into view again, this time as if it were actually happening in the present moment. I imagined that, rather than attending some women's gathering, which had sounded suspicious, Kirsten had somehow found out about Jilly and was at that moment packing herself and the kids up to leave. I felt a blind terror grip my heart. I wanted to get up and ride straight home to make sure everything was all right. "How do you know what to focus on, though?" I asked in a voice quivering with panic.

"Your true nature and purpose," Kaye sang out.

"Your true nature and purpose?" I groaned with dismay. The path of my salvation was beginning to sound more and more beyond me.

"That's right," said Kaye brightly. "You didn't come to earth to take a few hostages and hole up in the country.

That's not you; that's not your purpose in life. You've got to go after what you really want life to be about."

"What do you mean, hostages?" I asked in bewilderment. Reversing my fortune by the process Kaye was advocating now seemed so complicated. It sounded like years of self-discovery, when it felt like I had only hours or, at most, days to undo the damage I had wrought. I didn't have time for the luxury of self-discovery.

"Let me tell you something about human nature, Mark." Kaye shifted on her boulder to face me. She was as calm as I was agitated. "We're on the road to the most beautiful palace you can imagine. And here's the thing — this is the weird thing about humans: we keep stopping at the side of the road to build hovels, and we confuse these hovels with the palace we're heading for.

"We find something in life that gives us energy, and then we begin to act as if it's our only source of energy. Then we get possessive of that source. We want to protect it; we start hoarding it. Just like you, Mark. You've found a beautiful, warm, loving woman who's given you two lovely children, and you've created an occupation for yourself that pays you a reasonable living. And you've turned those things into your hovel. You've become stuck on them. You're insisting they are the only things that can give you life.

"When you came across magic, you got really excited because you thought it was a tool for propping up your energy source. But you see, magic isn't a way of fixing up your hovel; it is a life force that keeps you on the road to your palace, that allows you to keep your heart open to the abundance of the universe. Magic allows you to receive the plenitude of energy freely available from an unlimited number of sources."

Kaye said all this in the most placid tone, so I was taken by surprise when she suddenly became abrupt with me. "What happened with the meditation last night?" she snapped almost accusingly.

"Um... er... the meditation?" I stammered. "Yeah, no, it was amazing. It was terrific. Such peace and serenity, I can't even describe how great it was. It felt like I was back in the womb. Pity that state of mind isn't permanent."

"But it is, Mark!" cried Kaye, as if I'd just missed a free kick in front of the goal. "That's the thing: it is. You see, every state of mind exists in you simultaneously, from the sublime to the horrific. Whichever state of mind you focus on is the one you experience. That meditation I taught you is just a trick to bring your focus to a higher vibration. But the underlying structure in your consciousness doesn't permit your attention to stay there. Because your mind has been told that holding your family together is the primary purpose of life, and that keeping your business running is the key to achieving that, it keeps wandering back to check on how it's all going. And when it sees that those aspects of your life aren't as you believe they need to be, your mind starts to freak out. It's like a watchdog trained to alert you to a specific type of trouble. Except it doesn't bark; it creates an emotional pain that demands resolution.

"Now, just imagine that holding your family together and making your business work aren't the primary goals in your life. Imagine that being alive is your primary purpose. Not *surviving*, but just being alive and enjoying the wonder of life in all its aspects and forms. Imagine being a traveler through time and space, with freedom and adventure as your goals. Imagine the bliss you experienced last night being your goal. Imagine what your general state of mind would be then. It would be the end of suffering, wouldn't it? Not the end of pain, or grief, or disappointment, or frustration, or anger. But the end of suffering, because suffering is caused by attachment and trying to avoid loss."

I could smell the ease and freedom Kaye was talking about, but I couldn't see how I could have it. "Kaye," I objected politely, "that's all well and good for you. I have a wife and two kids, though. I'm responsible to someone who sacrificed her education and means of making a decent living to make a family with me, and to two children who can't provide for themselves. I can't just throw in the towel and go backpacking around the world. What state of mind would I enjoy if I knew I'd neglected the ones I love, the ones I'm morally and emotionally obliged to care for?"

"Good speech, Mark," Kaye clapped her hands in lighthearted mockery. "But you know what? You've just articulated the very cause of poverty consciousness. That noble, misguided sentiment you express is the illusion that creates poverty and misery on earth. Somehow or other, the human race has colluded to create the idea that life is about something other than living for ourselves. We've got to be responsible providers, achieve, succeed, become famous, look good, be great lovers, and sacrifice ourselves. Whose

bloody life is it, though? That's all our conditioning. It's all
for someone else. It's all about getting stuck on some objective and occupying your time with that while life passes you
by. Society holds out a meaningless objective and says, 'This
is the point,' and we blindly attach ourselves to it. You see,
now it's the family responsibility point; and when that's not
the point anymore, it'll be preparing for retirement, and
then death. You'll be asking yourself, 'Can I afford my own
funeral?' What sort of life is that? I mean, how much joy
can you squeeze out of such a petty existence?"

Kaye stopped talking. She looked sort of bewildered, as
if she didn't quite know where she was or how she had gotten there.

"So what is the point?" I asked her, hoping it would help
her refocus.

"The sixth secret of magic," said Kaye regaining her
composure. "You get your energy from a higher source."

"That's it?" I wasn't sure whether she had told me the
secret yet.

"That's it," she nodded. "Magicians aren't stuck on any
point. Their purpose is to live, to be open to the wonder of
life. Magicians aren't magicians because of what they can
conjure; magicians are magicians because of their ability to
be present. They're able to receive the blessing of life in
every moment. They can go with the flow of life and receive
their energy wherever and in whatever form it's being presented.

"You see, Mark, we all came here to live. For ourselves.
To be given the unique life the universe had in mind for us

personally. Having friends and family and fame and success, of whatever kind, is only incidental to being alive and enjoying the wonder of life. Sure, we get a lot out of our friends and families and our interests and achievements, and we love to put our hearts into them. But they're not our only sources of energy. They're not what we owe our first allegiance to. We owe our first allegiance to life. When you wake up to that, you're going to be elevated to a whole new experience of living.

"Life gave you your family and friends and successes and passions. And when those things aren't there, life has just as much energy for you in some other form. You just have to be awake to that truth."

Kaye's argument sounded appealing to me, inspiring even, but something held me back from buying it. "You make it sound as if the things I love and aspire to are wrong," I said, expressing my reservation. "You make it sound like I should give up my family and my possessions and wander around aimlessly — like life should be aimless, and in that aimlessness I'll find my fulfilment."

Kaye burst out laughing. "Not at all," she cackled. "Oh my God, that's so funny. You're obviously not getting it. Look, it's not about giving anything away; it's about not hanging on. There's a big difference. What I'm saying is that no one should sacrifice themselves for anyone else. You shouldn't have to provide for anyone else at the expense of your own destiny. You shouldn't have to provide for your family in the manner they've become accustomed to by being stuck in something that doesn't bring you any joy.

That's not serving you, is it? You should be doing something you love, and then whatever that brings in should be good enough for your family. You should all be able to get love and life and energy out of wherever that takes you.

"You are so afraid that if you let go of what you're doing now and begin something you're really passionate about, it wouldn't be good enough for everyone else. Like, if you went back to the city, you wouldn't be able to buy where you'd want to live, so you wouldn't be able to reflect the standing you did before. Big deal! What's the difference? Does your worth and enjoyment of life rise or fall on whether you own a house? You own a magnificent property now; does that make you happy? You say that if you sell your country place now you'll realize a big loss. What's the point in not realizing your loss if avoiding it is going to make you miserable and cost you everything in the end anyway? Can't you see how unreal and ridiculous your stance is? Why not just cut your losses and move on to the next thing waiting to give you energy? Why not go somewhere where there's action and passion and joy for all of you?"

I couldn't absorb all of what Kaye was saying and think at the same time. I just looked at the ground, waiting forlornly for her to continue.

"Because you don't know what that move will mean, that's why. You don't know what direction Kirsten will take if you go back to the city. You don't know how much you'll be able to offer materially. And you think you've got it under control where you are. Despite the suffering, you know where you stand.

"So let me ask you another question. What's the point in having the facade of a great life if you don't actually have a great life? What use is the shell if it has no substance? I mean, you've got the great manor out here in this gorgeous countryside. But who ever visits you out here? When do you guys have any fun? When aren't you sitting in your office biting your nails with worry? Why not give away the semblances of happiness and prosperity and actually live a rich, joyful life?"

By this time, Kaye had thoroughly enrolled me in how unappealing my life actually was. The thought of trying to keep it going another day exhausted me. I could see now what my striving had concealed from me. It really was all over. Whether it happened today or in a year's time, the end was inevitable. But this didn't stop me from making a last-ditch stand against Kaye's undeniable argument. "But what if I really focused on the business and got our income stream up to a comfortable level; then it'd be different, wouldn't it?" I postulated.

That started Kaye laughing heartily again. "Jesus, Mark, you never give up, do you? No wonder you're a good salesman. Phew!" She shook her head in disbelief. "Don't you get it? Selling business information is over. I didn't introduce you to magic so you could do your job ten times better; I did it to empower you to move on. Because no matter how brilliantly you stave off the inevitable, no matter how adroitly you cope with a dying industry, you can't change the fact that it's dying. I'm not here to help you defy the reality of life. I'm here to help you flow with the reality of life. To use change to move on to bigger and better things."

"That would be easy if it were just me," I remarked.

"Oh, don't talk crap," said Kaye lovingly. "You and your 'But I've got a wife and two kids.' Honestly, Mark, it's getting boring. You might like to think it's your job to protect everyone else, but it's not. That's the universe's job, same as it takes care of you. You may give some high and mighty reason about why you can't let go of the things you're attached to, but that's just a lie. The truth is, you're afraid that what you'll be left with won't be good enough for everyone else, and that if it's not good enough for them they'll abandon you. And the thing about that fear is that it's untested. You don't know how things will be, or how everyone will react to your new circumstances. You're being guided only by your assumptions. Your fears and beliefs are dictating your actions.

"And you know what? Even if your assumptions are correct, wouldn't it be better to be left standing alone than living a lie? Wouldn't you actually prefer it if all the things that weren't inherently connected to you fell away? Why do you want to waste your energy on people and things that aren't truly a part of you? Why do you want to reinforce your unworthiness by begging for love from those who don't really love you? Why not let all the shaky stuff fall away and create space for what's inherently connected to you, so you can rebuild on a solid foundation?

"They're waiting for you out there, you know — the people who are truly meant to give you love, and the things that are really going to make you happy. Just like Digby Wallace was waiting to give you that windfall. You just have to go out there with the expectation that it will happen, and this expectation will draw in everything that truly belongs to you. Same as the meditation technique. Expect the energy from the higher source, and it will come."

Kaye finished on a note so serene it felt almost ethereal, a quality strongly at odds with the harshness of the day. All living creatures had melted away to avoid the scorching sun. Only the rugged terrain around us was brave enough to show itself. My own mood reflected the bleakness of the insufferably hot summer morning.

"You know how I feel?" I confessed to Kaye. "I feel like I've been given a death sentence. Like a doctor has just given me three months to live. He has shown me the X-rays and the blood tests. All the evidence is there. There's no doubt I'm going to die. And that's all I can see. I can't see life after death. I can't see heaven or hell. Only me not here anymore in these beautiful hills, with my beautiful wife and my beautiful little angels."

"Yeah, but that's only because you're untrained in looking ahead," said Kaye, as cool as an alpine stream. "People are totally conditioned to look at what they stand to lose. They're so used to focusing on the dimensions they've defined as their energy sources that they can't see anything else. They've been living in the hovel so long they don't recognize the darkness in their lives as the shadow of the palace looming over them. But when you learn to look ahead instead of backward, you'll be so enamored of what you see, you won't think twice about letting the old dimensions go. If you surrender to life and go with it, you'll find it's an evolutionary process. As you move forward, so too do you evolve. You graduate to higher and higher levels of existence. Life becomes more and more joyful.

"For humans stuck in the old paradigm, losing anything is always a disaster, a terrible fate to be avoided at all costs. But to the magician, loss is merely an opportunity to create a higher structure. Magicians don't try to prop up a crumbling structure. They recognize problems as a sign that the underlying structure no longer serves them. They see the problem as an opportunity to create a higher, more sustainable structure. And really, ultimately, it's about going within. The more you let go of the external, the higher the structure you create. That state of mind you enjoyed last night: that was probably the highest you've been since you were a child, and it came from within you — nothing outside you can give you that.

"When you say you can't see anything, that's because you're looking in the wrong place. You're looking outside yourself. And of course, if we take your external props away from you, it's going to be bleak on the outside; it's going to be empty. But if you come back to yourself, you'll find your heart. And to be nurtured and oriented by your own heart is the most glorious thing possible. It's the sweetest, most fulfilling, most joyful, blissful way to be. When you look there, Mark, you'll see everything."

Kaye had emphasized the word *everything*. I looked at her in amazement. Who was this person sitting on the rock opposite me? Certainly I recognized the poised, almost delicate feminine form, but the sage-like personality who spoke through her was someone I never imagined existed. Just the power of her words astonished me. I felt like I had in the Bull Market when I'd fallen out of my head and dropped into my heart. What Kaye said had taken me straight back there. I suddenly realized there was someone inside my body, a light, energetic being dying to run wild in the world. A being full of passion and joy. A spirit unconcerned with outer form or social conventions, hierarchies, or standing. Someone who longed only to be in touch with that feeling of aliveness and to share it with the world. I sat there marveling at how simple my heart was and how easy it was to have it. It was as if all my life I had been putting on layer after layer of clothing until I was suffocating to death, and now I remembered I could just as easily take the layers off. And having stripped them off, I realized that being naked was better.

I was so enthralled by the buzz I gained by stepping outside my hovel, as Kaye might have put it, that I didn't even hear her begin talking again. I was mesmerized by the details of the world around me. Some part of me must have known I'd be interested in what she was saying, though, because I came back just in time to hear: "And the thing is, Mark, your gift is that you're excited by other people's passions. You know what they love, and it gives you great joy to share in their pursuit of that. You were born to help people know their hearts and to support them as they go for that. You're a guide — that's your nature. And your purpose is to fulfill that nature. You're the man who keeps everyone on the road and leads them to their palaces. That's where your bliss lies, my friend."

Hearing those words was the best thing that had ever happened to me. I couldn't express how right they sounded. I'd never thought of myself as a guide before, but when Kaye said it, it was as if I'd suddenly realized what I'd always known. I had already connected with the being within me and with its vibrancy and power. Kaye's acknowledgment was like an invitation to that being to channel that energy into the function it was designed to serve. My spirit had been given life. It had been awakened. Happiness! Joy! Excitement! But not even these words could describe the return of life where there was none before.

"You're right, Kaye," I said in reply. "What you say really rings true for me. But I've never had an experience of doing that. In fact, when I came back from the city, I thought I'd turn Kirsten on to the magic I'd learned — you know, get her passionate about moving on to a more empowered level. It kind of just sent her deeper into her swing circle, though." There was no pain in what I said. It was just light, matter of fact.

"Ah, well," said Kaye, "that's the last lesson you need to learn, the seventh secret of magic. Number seven, the sacred number: It takes will."

"It takes will?" Again, I wasn't sure whether that was the secret.

"That's right, will." Kaye said the word *will* as if she were in love with it. "Will is what the alchemists referred to as the philosopher's stone. That's what turns the lead into gold. Lead represents the lower vibration, and gold the higher. Will is the mechanism by which you assign the power in your consciousness. You use your will to take your attention off the lower vibration and hold it on the higher vibration. Will holds the new structure in place.

"You see, when you got home you were all excited about magic; you were focused on a higher vibration. Then you encountered Kirsten's negativity, which you let invalidate your vision. You assumed you'd have to come down to her level to deal with her. Your attention went from the higher to the lower again. The thing you need to know about magic is that whenever you go from a lower vibration to a higher vibration — or structure, if you will — more often than not it will look as if it's not going to work, especially when it involves others. People don't change their attitudes instantly, so if you judge how you're doing by other people's attitudes, you'll be disappointed very quickly.

"You have to learn temperance. Temperance is the ability to be okay when things do not change immediately. Nothing ever does. The impurities have to be burned off first. Like when someone gives up drugs: things feel worse to begin with while the body's chemical balance sorts itself out. The more meaningful a creation is to your heart, the more commitment it takes to stay with it. You make the decision to have what you love, and then stick with that choice. It's all too easy to give away the dream of your heart and buy into the reality of your mind or, even worse, other people's minds. Will is the ability to keep your dreams alive, to keep seeing them as reality."

"So where do you get a job as a guide?" I laughed, happy at how it felt to be in my lighter self.

"Nowhere." Kaye became uncharacteristically grave. "There are no institutional guides. You just have to allow your purpose to unfold. You have to decide that it's what you want, and wait for it to come. Live with the expectation of it coming, and then take the obvious action as it presents itself."

I didn't know why Kaye had taken me so seriously. To be honest, I wasn't worried about the how. I could see clearly who I was and what I really wanted. What amazed, surprised, and delighted me in that moment was the realization that I did know, and that I had decided that this was what I was now going to make my life about. It was like coming to terms with the conscious decision to live as an outlaw.

And now that I knew what I wanted, the how didn't matter. Considerations of how were only a device to stop me from moving on before I was ready to let go. Now that I had let go, I was past the point of no return, and the main reason the how didn't matter anymore was because I already had what I wanted: my heart! Whatever else was tied to that, and whatever form those things took, was incidental. All I cared about now was that I kept my spirit flying like a kite.

It struck me that I hadn't understood my golf lesson until now. The whole time, I'd been thinking that what Steve had taught me was to focus on the target, but I now realized that what he'd really taught me was to focus on the *right* target. There's a big difference!

In golf you can think that perfecting your swing is the target, but the flag is the true target. When I came home from the city, I mistakenly perceived the target as being all the things I believed I had to have in place before I could have my heart. I thought I had to make sure everyone perceived me positively, that I had to cultivate an unswervingly loyal and loving group of people around me, and set myself up in the most idyllic environment. And I'd been working on these targets as manically as I'd worked on perfecting my golf swing over the previous twenty years. I'd come back from the city thinking I'd been empowered to make those misguided priorities work, when in truth I was empowered to let them go and concentrate on my heart.

"Want a lesson in will?" asked Kaye.

"Okay," I replied.

"Let's ride down to the waterfall and cool off." Kaye got to her feet stiffly.

"What?" I groaned. "We'd have to ride all the way down the pass and then ride up the valley again. That's at least ten miles."

Kaye finished stretching her hamstrings before she replied. "When I rode up here last year, some boys showed me a shortcut." She smiled nonchalantly.

10 THE MAGICIAN'S WAY

Only a short distance from the lookout, Kaye stopped beside a firebreak that cut diagonally across the valley wall down toward the waterfall. "Is this it?" I asked in dismay, looking askance at the rugged track plunging down the steep mountainside. It wasn't a path I would have felt safe negotiating on my hands and knees, never mind on a bicycle. To even call it a path was an abuse of the English language. It was merely a swath of mountainside cleared of trees. All the boulders and gullies and soil-eroded corrugations with dead branches fallen across them were still there in their pristine condition.

"This is it," said Kaye enthusiastically. "We'll be swimming in five minutes."

"Are you sure you want to go down there?" I said, hoping my pessimism might shake her resolve.

"Are you sure you want to be a magician?" she asked without hesitation. "You've had all the insights, but you still have to learn to translate them into reality through action. Come on!" And she was off, rattling down the track at breakneck speed.

I began riding gingerly after her with my heart jumping into my throat every three seconds as my bike skidded and bumped its way down, continually threatening to send me flying over the handlebars or plunging down the ravine we were traversing. I didn't know how Kaye did it; she went flying down ahead of me. I was so frantically focused on negotiating all the stumps and potholes and branches and treacherous ledges that standing still would have been too fast for me.

Soon the inevitable happened. One too many obstacles jumped out at the same time, and I went over with a big thud. Cursing Kaye, I picked myself and my bicycle up and tried walking the bike down the hill. But it was too steep and awkward. I was forced to climb back on and continue my nerve-racking, two-wheeled descent. When I finally caught up with Kaye, she was waiting for me on the other side of a deep gully that cut across the firebreak.

"How did you get across there?" I asked, seething.

Kaye cocked her head at a big tree trunk spanning the gully on the uphill side of the track. "You have to ride up high along the bank and then ramp onto it above the roots," she said as casually as if she were telling me how to work an Instamatic camera.

"Are you crazy?" I swore at her. The thought of riding across a log as high above the ground as the rooftop of my house made me weak in the knees. I climbed off my bike and, registering my protest with a string of profanities, began carrying it across the tree trunk. The energy I had for cursing Kaye was soon diverted into balancing for my life. I began calling out, "Holy Jesus, Holy Jesus!" instead as I inched my way awkwardly over what to me felt like a broomstick spanning the Grand Canyon.

As soon as I'd made it across safely, my indignation returned with a vengeance. "Jesus Christ, Kaye," I fumed, "you're a maniac! We could die on this trail."

"Not the way you ride," she laughed, disregarding my crabby temper. "The only thing we'll die of on this mountain is old age if you keep riding so slowly."

"Stuff you," I growled.

"Hey, Mark," Kaye sang out blithely, "you're trying too hard. You're too focused on all the obstacles. This trail's too hard for that. There's too much going on for your body and mind to cope with. You have to hand things over to your natural ability if you want to ride down this trail." And with that she was off again, flying downhill as effortlessly as if she were riding down the bank of a velodrome.

"Ah, double stuff you!" I called out after her. "You know what? Triple stuff you!" When I got back on my bike and began riding, though, I could see exactly what Kaye had been talking about. My mind had been so taken up with trying to cope with the myriad hazards littering the pathway that I hadn't even been looking where I was going. Now I allowed myself to shift my focus to where I wanted to go and kept my attention on the line I was taking. Lo and behold, my experience went from one of struggling with a cumbersome mechanical contraption to one of riding on the back of a seemingly conscious beast. I was instantly transported from an excruciating, terrifying ordeal to an effortless joyride.

In no time at all, I was ramping over logs and rocks and letting myself fly down the track faster and faster. I was soon so confident I began clamping on my back brakes whenever I hit gravel for the sheer thrill of feeling the back wheel sliding out from under me.

Then suddenly I was flying toward a very sharp corner, and instead of thinking where I wanted to go, I thought of what would happen if I didn't take the corner. I realized that the bike wasn't following the line of the corner, and instead of leaning into it more I tried turning with my handlebars. When I felt that this wasn't doing the trick, I hit the brakes hard. Unluckily for me, I hit the front brake. As my front wheel dug into the ground, my back wheel flipped into the air, sending me flying over the handlebars. I landed heavily on my left side a good few yards down the track and went sliding across the gravel patch into a boulder on the verge of the downhill bank.

I lay there feeling nothing but disbelief. I didn't want to move for fear of discovering what damage I'd done to myself. I could feel something wet under my leg, and I knew it must be blood. I didn't even want to open my eyes.

I heard Kaye come running back up the hill. "Whoa! My God, what happened?" I couldn't believe it, but she was actually laughing. I heard her feet crunching past me on the gravel, and after a while she said, "Well, your bike's okay."

That made me open my eyes. Immediately blood ran into my left eye. "Don't worry about me," I moaned.

"First things first," said Kaye, standing my bike against a rock nearby. "Your bike's the only way we have of getting you off this mountain."

"What do you mean?"

"You'll see." Kaye reached out a hand to help me to my feet. Fueling my worst fears, she cried out, "Oh my God!" as I stood up.

My bicycle shorts and T-shirt were ripped to shreds all along the left side of my body. All the skin had been grazed off my outer thigh and outer upper arm and shoulder. Kaye confirmed that there was a gash above my left eye. "Might need a couple of stitches," she mused out loud. But apart from feeling a little bruised, the only discomfort I felt was the air stinging my grazes. More than anything I was stunned by the suddenness with which I'd lost control.

"Come, I'll show you the way down from here," said Kaye. She wheeled my bicycle for me while I limped along beside her. We didn't have far to walk. Kaye's bike was leaning against a rock wall just a few feet above where the firebreak ran over a cliff. She leaned my bike up against the wall beside hers and walked to the edge of the cliff. "Looks like we just ran out of road," she chuckled.

"So where's the way down?" I asked, failing to see any way around the cliff face.

"Straight over the edge."

"What?"

"Yeah, seriously, if you come and look over the edge

here, you'll see there's a kind of chute you can ride down."
Kaye beckoned me over.

I walked warily to the edge of the cliff. My body was
beginning to quake at the thought of looking down, and I
tried to peer over without actually standing on the edge. I
kept imagining the ground crumbling under my feet or a
gust of wind blowing me over, and feeling the sensation of
plummeting to my death.

"Here, hold on to me." Kaye put her arm out for me to
grab.

I shuffled fearfully to the brink of the rocky ledge we
were standing on, and, taking a deep breath, I forced myself
to look down. The whole world seemed to spin around 360
degrees, and when it came to a stop, I was looking down a
drop of what appeared to be the equivalent in height of an
inner-city high-rise. I gripped Kaye's shoulder for support
as my stomach became hollow and my legs turned to jelly.

"You see, everywhere else is just a sheer drop," Kaye
shouted as if she were calling out to someone at the bottom
of the cliff, "but here where it's granite, it hasn't been worn
away so completely. There's a slight gradient. The first ten
feet is 90 degrees, but then you catch the gradient and you're
actually running on both wheels from there. Then it's only
twenty or so feet down to that shoulder; and you can't see
it from here, but once you go over the shoulder it's a drop
of only another ten feet or so, and you're down. It looks
pretty rugged, but there's this groove here that's been
smoothed by running water. If you stay in that, you'll be
okay."

Hearing Kaye speak was like being in math class at school — I knew the teacher was talking, but I wasn't listening, because it wasn't anything I could wrap my head around. I looked up from the rock face to the foliage screening the valley and waterfall from our view. Logically, I knew we weren't that far from the valley floor, because the trees growing below rose up in front of us and towered high above our heads. Still, asking me to ride off the equivalent of a four-story building felt the same as asking me to jump out of a plane without a parachute.

"You really have to let yourself go on this one," Kaye shouted out again, to the imaginary person down below. "You'll be flying when you hit the pathway going into the forest, and it's going to twist and turn too quickly for your mind to respond. All you can do is imagine yourself coming out the other side of the woods and then hand yourself over to your natural ability. If you let your mind come in for even a split second, you're gone."

Standing at the edge of the cliff, I was too paralyzed by my fear of heights to feel anything. Once we'd moved back, though, and Kaye was straddling her bike and tightening her helmet, my mental and emotional faculties began restoring themselves. More than the fear of riding down the cliff face (I didn't have any intention of doing it), the main thing I felt was a strange sense of violation, a sadness that someone who was supposedly my friend, and who allegedly loved me, would trick me into such a cruel and perilous predicament.

"What are you waiting for, mister?" Kaye sang out with cheerful excitement.

"I'm not doing it, Kaye," I said.

"Of course you are!" she scoffed.

"I'm not."

"How do you think you'll get out of here?"

"Same way I came."

"You're kidding, Mark," Kaye cried out in disbelief. "It'll take you ages to climb up again. You'll die doing it in this heat. Soon the stiffness from your fall is going to set in, and when your grazes dry they're going to really hurt when you walk. Imagine trying to haul yourself and your bike across that tree trunk in your condition."

"I don't care, Kaye," I rejoined adamantly. "I'm not going down that cliff."

"Okay," said Kaye, resigning herself to my obstinacy. "You don't have to ride down with me. But can you do me just one favor?"

"What?"

"Ask yourself, fears aside, which way do you wish you could go down?"

"Well, of course it would be nice to go down this way," I sneered. "It would be nice if I could fly, too. But that's not going to happen, is it?"

"All right, maybe that was the wrong question," conceded Kaye in a conciliatory tone. "Just tell me what you're assuming."

"That I'll die if I go down there," I shouted hysterically. "But that's not an assumption, Kaye; that's a fact."

"Bullshit!" The word was like a slap in the face. "Bottom line is, you're assuming you can't trust your natural ability. It's not a fact that you'll die if you go over the edge. I've done it and lived. What's more, a couple of teenage kids showed me how.

"Up at the lookout, I could feel how alive you were, how in touch with your spirit you were. You were promising yourself that from now on you were going to live for your spirit. Then the first fear you face, and it's 'Sorry, spirit, but life's too dangerous to let you go where you want to. We've got to listen to fear. He's the boss.' You've frozen up again. But I'm telling you, Mark, there's nothing for you up that path. There won't be a single thing you want at the end of it. Everything you want lies where your heart wants to go."

There was no conciliation in Kaye's voice now. She sounded more like a prosecutor reading out damning charges. "You're right to think I'm not your friend. I'm not here for you right now; I'm here for your spirit. And just for once, I want you to listen to your soul. You don't even have to agree with it. I just want you to acknowledge which way it wants to go."

I felt as if Kaye's words had split my skull open and let my spirit out again. There was no denying where it wanted to go. I could feel my life force tugging me gleefully toward the cliff face. Despite some resistance that remained in me, I imagined the thrill of flying down the rock face and rocketing through the forest.

"You see, that's will, Mark," said Kaye more softly now. "Will is the mechanism by which we keep in touch with our heart, with our spirit. We don't ever think we have a choice in life. We don't consider that there's something beyond what we think and feel. We don't want to open up to hear what our heart is saying for fear it's going to contradict our mind, make us take the scary way. True limitation isn't a lack of money or having small ambitions; true limitation is the illusion that we lack options, that we lack choice. You're acting like you don't have a choice here. But you do. You just don't want to see that choice. And that's what will is: allowing yourself to see what choice your heart is giving you, and then actually going with that choice.

"I've seen a lot of people do all kinds of self-help and personal development work, thinking that the insights they gain into themselves will change them. But when it comes down to it, they don't have the will to take the action necessary to effect the change they're seeking. You see, there's always a void to step into, but usually it's not as obvious as this one. It might be telling someone an uncomfortable truth or going against popular opinion, or it might be taking on a task you don't feel up to. And the problem is, you don't know what going through with it means; your only certainty lies in not going through with it. Like here, even though it would be a struggle to haul your bike up the firebreak, and even though you would get little return for your effort, you would know what to expect. Your survival would be assured.

"And that's the path most people take. Ninety-eight percent of humans use their minds to follow their thoughts and feelings and keep their hearts locked out. But that's not the magician's way. The magician's way is through the void. Magicians don't understand their hearts, but they know that their hearts will never lead them anywhere that isn't ultimately for their highest good."

Kaye beamed. "It all depends on whether you're satisfied with your hovel or you're going for your palace. If you want your palace, follow your heart. Everything you truly love lies in the direction your heart wants to go." She began pedaling slowly toward the edge of the cliff. "Remember the trick of the mind," she called out, as a reminder more to herself, I felt, than me. And then she fell out of sight with a shriek that followed her down the cliff face and all the way through the forest. There was a brief silence, and then an intelligible scream of victory resounded through the valley. I imagined I could hear the faint sound of cheering and clapping.

The valley went still again. I looked down at my legs straddling my bicycle. I couldn't believe I was about to ride down a vertical incline I didn't even have the nerve to look down. There was a piercing cry, and the eagle we'd seen up at the lookout came sailing low over my head. This time I fancied I caught a glint of respect in its eye, as if it now recognized me as a fellow aviator.

A big part of me fully expected to die. I looked at the world around me wistfully, as if for the last time. I felt myself choking up at the thought of not being part of life. Yet in spite of that despondency, I was still fully conscious of the outcome I wanted. All I pictured was myself coming out of the forest in one piece.

With every fiber in my body and brain screaming for me not to do it, I began pedaling, zombie-like, toward the cliff face. The first shock was the sensation of the front wheel falling away. Every form of consciousness fell away from me with it, save pure terror. I was screaming so mightily I was already going over the granite shoulder before I realized my wheels were touching the ground again. There wasn't even a split second for me to be thankful for surviving the first thirty feet of the drop before I was virtually hanging upside down again with the earth flying up toward my face.

Somehow I survived a massive speed wobble at the bottom of the cliff, only to find myself flying along a narrow path that apparently led straight into an immense tree trunk. Only when I was nearly on top of the huge tree did I notice the path opening up to go around it. I threw myself desperately to the left, with no objective other than to avoid hitting the tree head-on. I clipped the tail end of one of its tentacle-like roots and went flying into the air almost on my side. With a desperate lunge, I managed to center myself just as my wheels hit the ground again. No sooner had I brought a bowel-loosening wobble half under control than the path veered sharply to my right.

And so I ricocheted through the forest like an out-of-control rocket, shocked more than anything at surviving each near-wipeout. Only when I saw the pathway opening up into a long, straight avenue did it occur to me that maybe I should have used my brakes coming down the cliff. I had only a moment to imagine I was safe. Before I knew it, I was careening up an earthen ramp that culminated on the crest of a riverbank. Next thing, I was airborne for about the fifth time, on target to land in the middle of a broad, slow-running river.

I seemed to fly through the air in slow motion. Instantly, I realized that a soft landing was assured — I had made it. And in that same moment my terror cut out, making way for the most incredible adrenaline rush. Each and every fiber that had been screaming for me not to commit suicide was now cheering with fervent appreciation. It seemed like I was being held aloft on wings of ecstasy. I took my hands off the handlebars and, raising my two clenched fists above my head, let out a roar of triumph that didn't let up even as I sank into the water.

The first thing I noticed when I surfaced was a bedraggled Kaye jumping up and down on the far bank, whooping and cheering. Unable to contain her enthusiasm, she dived back into the water and began swimming over to me. I didn't wait for her; instinct compelled me to save my precious mountain bike. I dived down to retrieve it. By the time I reached it, Kaye was there to help me bring it to the surface.

We awkwardly maneuvered the bicycle to dry land. We heaved it onto the bank and then stood there, looking at each other, both waiting for the other to say something. No words came. We were in a state of speechless euphoria. Our excitement could not be contained, though, and it bubbled out of our mouths as a fountain of laughter. The laughter rocked us off our feet, sat us down on our backsides, and racked our bodies until our sides hurt.

Finally, Kaye gave a mirth-filled sigh of content, wiped the tears from her cheeks, stood up shakily, and dived back into the deep water. I dived in after her. I let myself sink to the bottom of the river and allowed myself to receive the joy of the moment. It was as if I were floating in the thrill of life itself. I felt as though my physical body had washed away and what was left was a concentration of ecstatic energy. This energy had tentacles that reached out to, and communicated with, everything in the water and forest and sky around me. An unfamiliar sense of power surged through me, the sense that nothing could destroy my essence, and that I was receiving energy from everything in the universe. I had a feeling of delight, as if I'd come home to myself, and the world was happy to welcome me back.

Kaye and I lazed around in the water for a long time without speaking. We both knew that words would only detract from the sacredness of the moment. After what might have been five or ten minutes — but felt like an eternity — we pulled ourselves out of the water and sat beside each other on the bank, soaking up the heat of the midday sun, staring at the ripples of water dancing endlessly by us, and listening to the reassuring sound of the waterfall upriver.

Finally, Kaye looked at me with a pleasantly worn-out smile. "How was that?" she inquired.

"Just amazing." I shook my head in wonder, smiling back at her. "That was the most astonishing thing I've ever experienced. I can't believe I just did that."

Her smile widened, and as her eyes lit up in recognition, I had a flash of understanding.

"You know how, back on the mountain, you said that everything I wanted lay where my heart wanted to go? It's pathetic, I know, but a part of me held the feeble hope that what you meant was that if I made some dramatic gesture of faith, like going over the cliff, my life would be magically fixed. Like, maybe Kirsten and Jilly and Trevor and Steve would be down here to meet us, and you guys would reveal that the hell I've been through these last few weeks was all some setup to teach me what I truly needed to learn. It was a brief fantasy of magical peace and resolution, where I'd wake up to find that the past was forgiven, that everyone understood everything and I was safe again. I even thought I heard other people down here when you headed off before me. I was kind of disappointed to find you alone here."

A look of dismay began forming on Kaye's face.

"But coming down that cliff has changed all that — blown it away! Now I know what you meant when you said 'everything you want.' You know, Trevor taught me that everyone has a heart; well, what he didn't tell me was that every*thing* has a heart. Just this morning I remembered how, when I was a kid, I used to feel like everything in the whole world loved me and supported me, and for the first time in ages I feel like that again. Lying in the water just now, it felt like my spirit was being kissed by every rock and stone and bird and branch."

I looked around at the forest in wonderment as the realization of what I was saying hit me. "I feel like I truly understand what you've been teaching me, Kaye. Retreating back up the mountain really did represent my hovel, that shutdown world where I was fixed on the few people or things I believed were going to give me the forgiveness or approval or permission I needed to live. It's when I surrender responsibility for my life to this person or that job that I become separate and lose my connection to the heart and soul of my environment, to my own heart and soul."

Kaye turned to face me as I reached out and placed my hand on her shoulder. "I've got to tell you, I wanted to kill you up there on that ledge when you told me that the only way down was over the edge of the cliff. Now I don't know how to express my gratitude. How else would I have come into my power? How else would I have seen that nothing else is important compared to this freedom, that this is everything my heart really wants?"

Kaye sat there staring at the river, letting my words sink in. Then she absently said, "Kirsten? Jilly?" They were only two words, yet they embodied an entire counterargument.

I considered Kaye's rebuttal. "When I was giving Kirsten and Jilly and the Bull Market crew responsibility for my life, all I could see was the devastating power they had over me, how they could destroy me. I imagined that their disapproval could convince the rest of the world to turn against me, too. Now, though, when the power is in me and my connection to life, the thought of dealing with them doesn't overwhelm me.

"What I learned today was that there is no life in safety. Avoiding conflict or misfortune has only turned me into a shrunken shell of a person; being vulnerable has connected me to life again, and that's all I want now, Kaye — to be alive. Facing Kirsten and Jilly and my whole life circumstance is scary, believe me, but that's not going to stop me.

My heart is crying out to face the reality I've created. I'm ready now — keen, even."

As I spoke, Kaye became more animated. "Yeah," she added, excitedly, "that's the thing about magic: when you use it, it empowers you. You have an experience of its power, and that emboldens you to aim higher. It's almost like a law or principle of magic — the principle of momentum. Using your will doesn't only get you things; it also gives you the energy to go for even more."

I laughed in deference to Kaye's wisdom. "Where do you get all this stuff?" I asked.

"What do you mean?" she asked innocently.

"Well, these secrets, these laws, principles, whatever you call them — where did you learn them? From a book?"

"Not really," she said, frowning, as if she were contemplating this notion for the first time. "You find bits of it here and there. Magicians pass on what they know. There are no definitive writings on the subject." After a pause, she looked at me sharply and said, "Why, are you thinking of writing a book now?"

Nothing, of course, had been further from my mind. The idea of writing on any subject, let alone magic, seemed preposterous — until the moment Kaye expressed it. A brilliant emotion filled me with light, leaving no room for anything other than the certainty that this was what I had been born to do. For the first time in my life, I understood the meaning of words like *passion* and *inspiration* — that some things you just had to do because your heart demanded it, rather than because your circumstances dictated it.

In spite of my instant enthusiasm about the idea, I was guarded about what Kaye might think. "Come on, be serious," I protested. "What do I know about magic? I haven't even sorted out my own life yet."

"That could be the second book," she mused. "I was only kidding when I said it, but it rang true. I'm serious; I think revealing this magic to the world is your calling." She raised her eyebrows and nodded emphatically, urging me to agree.

I felt the ecstatic energy once again flare up and reach its tentacles out into the forest. A chorus of exquisite sensations sang approval of the idea. "It's just weird," I said, "like the earth opened up and swallowed the old me, and now there's another person sitting here in his place. I mean, everything I thought I was, everything I made my life about, has just been obliterated. I'm sitting here with a whole new meaning and purpose of life. The past that I hung on to for so long seems unreal."

"Well," exclaimed Kaye with delight, "that's how you know you're standing in the magician's world, not just sticking a straw into it." She leaped to her feet. "It's that bewilderment the Sufi poets talk about," she continued. "You have to lose yourself totally before you can come to your heart. The mind orients itself by sticking to what it knows from the past, whereas the heart gets its knowing from the moment. The heart steps outside the past to include all possibility. That's the only real truth, and you have to learn to love the disorientation that opens you to it; otherwise, you'll never be a magician."

As if to emphasize the finality of her pronouncement, Kaye turned her back on me, waded through the shallows, and dived into the deep water, leaving me to come to terms with my bewilderment.

I had always associated bewilderment with confusion and dread, but the space I was in at that moment was more like joy. Sitting there on the grassy bank, basking in the hot, life-giving rays of sunshine, I marveled at how empty I felt, how unattached I was to anything outside myself. I knew for certain that everything I thought and felt originated purely from within. This emptiness and freedom was me. Unable to contain my joy, I jumped up and followed Kaye into the water.

Out in the deep, I floated on my back, closing my eyes to shield them from the harsh sun. A raft of questions crowded into my mind: How would I resolve my relationship with Kirsten and the situation with Jilly? What would happen to my business? How could I write a book when I had no experience as a writer? I entertained my doubts for a while, but they soon became boring and I let them go. I chose instead to focus on what I loved. And when I did, it was as if everything I had become over a lifetime dissolved, and I was the spirit of a seven-year-old boy again, coming out of a thirty-year coma, ready to tear around in the world God had made for me to play in.

THE SEVEN SECRETS OF MAGIC

THE FIRST SECRET

Your thoughts and feelings aren't real.

Your thoughts and feelings are expressions of your underlying assumptions in any moment, not reflections of actual reality or what is truly possible.

THE SECOND SECRET

Your focus creates your reality.

Your experience in life is determined by what you put your attention on. If you focus on end results, you inevitably attract what you want. If you focus too much on what you have to do to get what you want, you end up attracting your doubts, fears, and beliefs.

THE THIRD SECRET

Everyone has a heart.

Having a heart means that you do have dreams, that there are things you love, things that are deeply important to you.

An inherent part of the human journey is that at some point you end up putting more energy into protecting your heart than following it.

THE FOURTH SECRET

There is never anything to do, but always action to take.

Action is about taking direct steps, based on the obvious, toward creating what you want. *Doing* is about fulfilling certain conditions you believe are necessary before you can get what you want.

THE FIFTH SECRET

Structure has integrity.

Something's structure dictates its behavior, and its behavior dictates its experience. In creative terms, what your attention is focused on forms the underlying structure of your consciousness. The motivations behind what you do in life reveal your true focus.

THE SIXTH SECRET

You get your energy from a higher source.

As a human being, you have the tendency to develop fixed concepts about what is in your highest good and where it is supposed to come from. The key to magic is developing the ability to let go of your fixed concepts and open up to the true source of your energy.

THE SEVENTH SECRET

It takes will.

Ultimately, your highest source of energy is your own heart. Yet the paradox is that you are conditioned to protect your heart, a behavior motivated by fear. Your fears are communicated to you by thoughts and feelings. There can be no sustainable change in your experience of life unless you have the will to choose following your heart over resolving your thoughts and feelings.

ABOUT THE AUTHOR

William Whitecloud's association with magic can be traced back to his childhood in the small African country of Swaziland, where he was immersed in the supernatural worldview of the tribespeople around him. This association was reinforced when he immigrated to Australia in 1983 and began speculating in global financial money markets, using profoundly esoteric methods for predicting market movements.

Over time William's attention shifted from observing phenomena at work outside himself to finding ways he could practically apply magic to creating what truly mattered to him in his own life. This search brought him into contact with the alchemical principles of Hermetic Philosophy and the ideas of Robert Fritz, founder of Technologies for Creating. Within months, William had begun to study and teach these superbly effective modalities for reconnecting with and manifesting what is truly important to the human spirit.

In 1996 William founded the Living from Greatness program, dedicated to empowering participants to discover and live their authentic natures and purposes. Through his involvement in the program, he has worked one-on-one with hundreds of individuals over periods of two to three years, coaching them in bringing their dreams into reality. His search to discern the essence of what it takes for people to connect with and live from their creative spirits forms the basis of this, his first book, *The Magician's Way*.

William lives in Byron Bay, Australia, one of the most creative and loving communities in the world, where he devotes his time to coaching, writing, enjoying his young family, and letting life unfold by magic.